PENGUIN BOOKS

FIGHTING FOOD

Marilyn Lawrence has worked as a psychiatric social worker and as a university lecturer. She began working with women with eating disorders when she was employed in the National Health Service and later set up a voluntary counselling service for anorexic women and their families in Leeds. She is involved in the educational work of the Women's Therapy Centre and has been an adviser to Anorexic Aid and a member of the council of the Eating Disorders Association. Her published works include *The Anorexic Experience* (1984), *Fed Up and Hungry* (1987) and, with Mira Dana, *Women's Secret Disorder* (1988). She now lives in London, where she works as a psychotherapist.

Mira Dana was born in Haifa, Israel. She took her BA in psychology and sociology and, during her university years, worked with veterans of the army and later in a psychiatric hospital with drug addicts. She came to England in 1977 after several months of travelling in Europe, and in London took her MA in humanistic psychology from Antioch University. At the same time, she completed her psychotherapy training at the Minster Centre. In 1979 she joined the Women's Therapy Centre, where she is a group and individual therapist and the co-ordinator for eating problems. She also runs workshops and supervises and trains people working with eating problems. She set up p.a.c.s. (post-abortion counselling service) and co-founded Perspective, an organization offering training and consultancy from a feminist perspective to women and men working in the caring professions. She also lectures in the UK and abroad.

FIGHTING FOOD
Coping with Eating Disorders

Marilyn Lawrence and Mira Dana

PENGUIN BOOKS

PENGUIN BOOKS

Published by the Penguin Group
27 Wrights Lane, London W8 5TZ, England
Viking Penguin Inc., 40 West 23rd Street, New York, New York 10010, USA
Penguin Books Australia Ltd, Ringwood, Victoria, Australia
Penguin Books Canada Ltd, 2801 John Street, Markham, Ontario, Canada L3R 1B4
Penguin Books (NZ) Ltd, 182–190 Wairau Road, Auckland 10, New Zealand

Penguin Books Ltd, Registered Offices: Harmondsworth, Middlesex, England

First published 1990
10 9 8 7 6 5 4 3 2 1

Copyright © Marilyn Lawrence and Mira Dana, 1990

The moral right of the authors has been asserted

All rights reserved

Filmset in 10½/12 pt Monophoto Ehrhardt
Printed in England by Clays Ltd, St Ives plc

Except in the United States of America, this book is sold subject to
the condition that it shall not, by way of trade or otherwise, be lent,
re-sold, hired out, or otherwise circulated without the publisher's
prior consent in any form of binding or cover other than that in
which it is published and without a similar condition including this
condition being imposed on the subsequent purchaser

Contents

    Introduction *vii*
1. What Are Eating Disorders? *1*
2. Anorexia *17*
3. Compulsive Eating *30*
4. Bulimia *44*
5. Women in the World *56*
6. Women's Psychology *76*
7. Boundary and Self *92*
8. Misconceptions and Common Approaches to Treatment *103*
9. Developing a Psychotherapeutic Approach *116*
10. Principles of Self-help *133*
11. Self-help in Practice *155*

    Finding Help *171*
    Bibliography *175*
    Index *178*

INTRODUCTION

The central aim of this book is to draw together recent developments in our understanding of eating disorders, and in particular to explore the connections between the different kinds of symptoms which individuals produce.

Our orientation is one which seeks to encompass both the individual and the social factors which together have produced such an alarming incidence of symptoms connected with food and eating. We attempt to describe, analyse and help with the current epidemic of eating disorders.

Both authors are psychotherapists, and we have been concerned in our work for many years to understand and help individuals with their difficulties and their lives. At the same time, we have struggled to make sense of what we were learning and understanding in terms of the particular developmental experience of women, growing up in contemporary society.

The Women's Therapy Centre has been central to this endeavour. It has provided not only the setting for much of the actual work, but, perhaps even more importantly, the space for thinking, discussing, arguing and gradually teasing out the themes as they have emerged. The Centre has occupied the unique position of trying to provide a service for women and at the same time working towards a new understanding of women's psychology.

Eating disorders and men

Throughout this book, we refer to eating disorders as though they were problems only for women. We know that this is not so. Some experts estimate that as many as one in ten anorexics are men, and we have met a few, though not many, bulimic men. Comparatively few men complain of compulsive eating and although many men do overeat, they tend not to regard it as a problem.

The overwhelming majority of people who suffer from eating

disorders are women, and one of the central questions which we set out to answer is why this should be so.

We look for the answer to this question in the complex interplay of social and psychological issues which affect women's lives. It is important to understand, though, that issues which are problematic for a great many women can also be so for some men. While we often emphasize the differences between the experience of women and of men, we are well aware that there are great and possibly growing areas of overlap. Men who develop eating disorders face many of the same conflicts and dilemmas as women with similar problems.

A number of the men we have met and worked with have told us how alienated they sometimes feel at the emphasis on women's experience in the literature on eating disorders. This book will not help that situation very much, but it is our hope that men will manage to disregard the constant references to 'she' and 'her' and will be able to identify with the human situations we describe.

There are a number of basic problems in writing a book about eating disorders, which is essentially a book about symptoms. One of these is the danger that symptoms will occupy the foreground of all discussion, with the actual people, renamed 'sufferers', appearing only as two-dimensional figures behind. An individual life can thus come to represent an example of 'bulimia'; an identity is lost, transformed instead into 'an anorexic'. In the same way, one can end up talking about 'women' as though all women are the same and share an identical history and experience.

We have tried to avoid creating new stereotypes and whenever possible we have placed individuals at the centre of the pictures we are drawing, letting them speak in their own words. We have then had to ask ourselves, given that there really is no such person as the 'typical compulsive eater', whether it is useful to make generalizations at all.

The result is inevitably a compromise. We *have* made generalizations, and often quite sweeping ones, especially in the chapters which focus on some of the underlying psychological issues and compare the ways in which they are expressed through the different eating disorders, but we have been at pains to give an account of the unique history of the individual whenever we can.

We have to ask the reader to play her or his part in this. The book can only be useful if the generalizations, the theoretical formulations, are seen and used as tools or, to use a different analogy, signposts, which can enable an individual to open up or find a sense of direction in understanding her own particular situation.

The women who appear in the pages which follow come from the widest possible diversity of backgrounds. It is often believed that women with eating problems, and especially anorexics, are 'middle-class'. It is now being recognized that this is simply not true. It is still often an implicit assumption that working-class women, poor women, while they may be overweight, do not really 'suffer' because of their eating disorder. Not only is this untrue, but it seems to us to be a clear instance of the professional prejudice which permeates much of the mental health services.

Black women and women from other minority groups are well represented among the women we have worked with. It is our fear that they are probably over-represented in the total number of women who actually suffer from eating disorders. Racism is a destructive pressure for black women, which makes the task of forming a positive identity even more problematic.

The final myth is that eating disorders are problems only for young women. Combined with this is the idea that women 'grow out of' eating disorders when they marry and have children. Our work has shown us time and time again that eating disorders can occur at any point within a woman's life and that motherhood is no guarantee of immunity or recovery.

This book is the culmination of many years of work with women with eating disorders. Our aim has been to do something entirely new: to put together what we have learned about anorexia, bulimia and compulsive eating with what we understand about women's psychology and development in a society which is still essentially patriarchal.

1
WHAT ARE EATING DISORDERS?

Millions of women throughout the western world suffer from what we have come to know as eating disorders. These problems cause untold distress for women, are frequently disabling and can sometimes be life-threatening. Yet for many people, such problems remain a mystery.

Most people nowadays have heard of anorexia nervosa, even if they have only the vaguest notion of what it is. It is also generally acknowledged that many people have a problem with overeating. In very recent years we have become familiar with a new form of eating disorder known as bulimia or bulimia nervosa, in which a person eats large quantities of food and then makes himself or herself sick or takes laxatives to get rid of the food.

It is difficult to make an accurate assessment of the number of people who suffer from eating disorders. They often go unreported and untreated, and most researchers are cautious about suggesting numbers. Nonetheless, it has been estimated that as many as one in every 200 young women suffers from the life-threatening disorder known as anorexia nervosa.[1] Vast numbers of women frequently resort to dieting, feeling themselves to be overweight; for many, life seems one endless struggle against eating 'too much'.[2] It is impossible to estimate the number of women who suffer from the secret symptom of bulimia nervosa,[3] but the evidence suggests that we have not yet seen even the tip of the iceberg.

We have reached a point where we take all these problems for granted and fail to be surprised that so many people have such profound and life-threatening difficulties with food, eating and the ability to nourish themselves appropriately and easily. But if we stop for a moment to consider the matter, it is by no means obvious why this should be so. Why does the most promising undergraduate in her year begin a relentless pursuit of thinness, apparently out of the blue, when no one has ever guessed she has a problem? What about the interesting, talented, successful young executive who for years fights a secret and lonely battle against her compulsion to make herself sick every day?

Eating is one of the most basic and fundamental human activities. Together with breathing, it is the one activity which is essential for human beings to survive. And yet, unlike breathing, it is an activity which is voluntary, in which the individual must actively participate. Even a tiny baby must take the positive step of sucking in order to find nourishment. So as well as being a fundamentally necessary human activity, eating requires a specific motivation and it is one over which we have a considerable amount of control.

Unlike air, food is not merely available all around us, waiting to be consumed. Human societies at all stages of their development devote a considerable amount of time and energy to the production and preparation of the food they eat. Food must be grown, which involves a vast investment in agriculture and animal husbandry; it must be gathered or hunted and it must be prepared and cooked.

For many artists and writers, a concept of paradise is one in which delicious food is completely available, where fruit falls from the tree, where sumptuous dishes appear as if by magic and where all the effort involved in self-nourishment is removed. That, however, is merely a fantasy. In reality, in order to eat, human beings must engage in an almost endless preoccupation with food. It is this preoccupation with food and eating which endows the activity with so many different meanings and associations for us. Eating is not just a routine activity, a reflex action; no one, apart from people threatened by famine and starvation, eats merely to live.

There are no societies we know of in which everyone eats everything which can be eaten. All of us have certain foods which we consider to be inedible, even though they may be eaten by neighbouring communities. England is, by almost any standards, a small island. Yet in the north, the jellied eel, much loved by southerners, has always been little more than a joke. Conversely, eating meat pie with mushy peas, liberally sprinkled with *mint sauce*, is quite an appalling idea in southern England, while it makes a tasty lunch in the north.

Both pie and peas and jellied eels are foods traditionally enjoyed by working-class people, and even in this tiny island they are largely unknown to the affluent. In our own society social class divisions are represented as much as anything else by the kinds of foods we eat. Whether it is fact or fantasy, we cling to the idea that working-class people eat different food from middle-class people; we associate 'left wing' with whole foods, muesli and vegetarianism, while caviar and game have aristocratic associations. The conspicuous consumption of large amounts of rich and rare food is always associated with affluence, and in many societies, including our own, the giving of feasts (or dinner parties) is a means of displaying power and wealth as well as generosity. When royal or state events are in the news the reporting often includes an account of the menus.

It is not just what we eat that marks us out as belonging to a particular social group, but how we eat it and what we drink with it. The incomprehensible mystique of culinary 'know-how' is summed up by the 'food' journalist in the *Guardian* newspaper: 'Nothing is more socially unacceptable than a solecism at table, whether it be ordering a pudding wine with the grilled sole or eating asparagus with a knife and fork.' This leads us to the suspicion that the north–south divide which separates the jellied eel eater from the person who prefers pie and peas is considerably less impermeable than the iron curtain between the classes.

If the possession and consumption of good food is a sign of favour and fortune, then refusing food also has its meanings. In some cultures to refuse hospitality is a grave insult, and even within modern Western culture a refusal of food is viewed with suspicion. If the guests refuse the chocolate mousse, the hostess is unlikely to feel pleased that they have already had enough and that she can freeze it for a future occasion. On the contrary, she may feel quietly angry and humiliated that no one will appreciate her efforts.

It is certainly true to say that, in the modern world, food is in many respects easier to acquire than it has been in the past. The supermarket makes shopping easier, and pre-packaged and prepared foods, together with radically different technologies for cooking, look as though they should make life easier for the housewife. In theory, she should spend less of her time concerned with the buying and preparation of food. In fact, of course, our expectations of what we take into our bodies have increased and changed. We are no longer satisfied to eat whatever foods are in season. We expect, and give ourselves, an almost infinite variety, defying nature and geography in our pursuit of more and better food. We not only demand quality and variety, but in addition we want healthy food, well cooked and pleasing to the eye.

The medical profession, as well as the vast food industry, encourages us to be discerning in what we buy, to choose one brand of food rather than another. Health considerations, so important in themselves, have been hijacked by the producers of food. The sensible research on the importance of 'fibre' has probably done more to improve the share prices of the baked bean canners than it has to enhance the nation's health. It seems extraordinary that 'no additives' and 'no added colouring' are now advertising slogans on the complex, sophisticated packaging in which we buy our foods. We could almost be tempted to forget that it was the food manufacturers, not the bemused housewife, who started colouring and preserving food in the first place!

Correspondingly, rather than a decrease in the demands made on women, the changes in our eating patterns and the vast range of choices and new considerations which now beset them have meant that women probably spend more time in the kitchen. The physical labour may be less, but feeding a family is now a serious business and it is time-consuming.

Within the cultural diversity which is now so much a part of daily life in the West, food takes on many meanings, collective and individual. Eating can express and symbolize powerful feelings. Food and eating express our sense of unity and our feelings of being different. What we eat delineates our social group and enables us to include and exclude each other. Love, caring and concern are expressed through food – by refusing to eat someone's food, we can make them feel our rejection without ever having to put it into words. People who develop eating disorders are effectively using food with its rich social imagery to express conflicts and feelings which they feel incapable of expressing in any other way.

What are eating disorders?

Perhaps the most useful way of defining an eating disorder is as any kind of eating which is not about satisfying physical hunger and which is or produces a problem for that individual. All of us, from time to time, eat for reasons other than physical need. No one eats their after-dinner mint because they are hungry! Equally, we may put off eating even when we are hungry, perhaps because we are going to the sports centre or for religious reasons, or even because we don't have time. This kind of behaviour, based on a decision, a choice, does not normally constitute or lead to a problem for the individual.

A person with an eating disorder does not experience herself as making a choice. She feels that her pattern of eating is dictated by something outside her conscious control. All eating disorders are characterized by distress in relation to food. It is not useful to think of eating disorders as the consumption of abnormal quantities of food; there is, after all, no 'correct' amount of food to eat, and individuals vary a great deal in how much food they need to stay healthy and satisfied. Many people *believe* that their problem is eating too much or too little food, but this is in fact merely an expression of the distress which surrounds food and eating.

Common to eating disorders is an obsession or preoccupation with food. The individual who develops an eating disorder is unable to identify hunger correctly or to distinguish it from other bodily needs or states of emotional arousal. Often feelings like anxiety, anger or sexual arousal are mistaken for hunger, while genuine 'stomach hunger' is misperceived or ignored altogether.

Perhaps the most common pattern of disordered eating is compulsive eating. Compulsive eating is sometimes, though not always, associated with overweight. Some women who are fatter than they would like to be do not eat compulsively, and many compulsive eaters maintain a weight they can accept by equally compulsive dieting. We would define as a compulsive eater any woman who eats when she really doesn't consciously mean or want to. This may take the form of a continuous 'picking' at different foods, without ever really having a proper meal, or it may on the other hand take the form of large, secretive 'binges'. Whatever the pattern of the compulsive eating, it is invariably followed by feelings of guilt and shame, frightening feelings of being out of control and a resolution to limit food intake in the future.

Many women who are compulsive eaters find their lives dominated by thoughts of food and by their own attempts to control their weight and food intake. A day will be judged 'good' or 'bad' according to how little or how much has been eaten, and the scales are continually consulted for signs of 'success' or 'failure'.

Anorexia nervosa is another form of eating disorder and at first sight looks the complete opposite of compulsive eating. The woman in an anorexic phase limits her food intake to the extent that she loses a vast amount of weight, ceases to menstruate and shows other physical signs of malnutrition. She is often extremely active, engaging in vigorous exercise and seeming oblivious to tiredness or discomfort. Her whole existence seems to revolve around the pursuit of thinness, and above all she is terrified of the very thought of gaining weight. Like the compulsive eater, she is preoccupied with control, and women with these symptoms live in fear of losing it. While on the surface compulsive eating and anorexia nervosa appear to be completely opposite kinds of problem, in the chapters which follow we shall see that they have a great deal in common.

Bulimia or bulimia nervosa is an eating disorder in which the central symptom is overeating followed by self-induced vomiting and sometimes purging with laxatives. Bulimic women invariably keep their eating disorder a secret, appearing to lead normal and often very successful lives. Most women who suffer from bulimia are not markedly over or underweight – no one would guess that they suffered from an eating disorder.

Some bulimic women overeat and make themselves sick perhaps once or twice a week; for others it is an almost constant preoccupation. It is not uncommon for women to make themselves sick as many as ten times a day and have little time, energy or money for anything else in their lives. We have spoken to a woman who, on her 'worst' day, vomited forty times. It is difficult to imagine that such a day would leave space for anything else at all, and we can only begin to imagine what psychological distress must be represented by this disturbed behaviour.

All eating disorders – compulsive eating, anorexia and bulimia – are extremely destructive both physically and psychologically. Compulsive eating often leads to obesity, and although doctors generally agree that mild overweight is not a hazard to health, extreme obesity certainly is. Anorexia can certainly be a life-threatening disease. A substantial minority of women in an anorexic phase do die, and many more might do so were it not for the concern of families and health care professionals. Bulimia exacts a hidden health toll. Digestive disorders, throat damage and devastation of the teeth (caused by the action of stomach juices on the enamel) are among the documented effects, and long-term vomiting or laxative abuse can deplete the body of essential elements with serious and life-threatening results.

Psychologically, eating disorders are perhaps even more serious and damaging. Time and again women confirm to themselves that they are bad, weak and powerless against food. Many anorexics waste years of their lives with their fruitless obsession, and as many again lead colourless half-lives, having appeared to recover following hospital treatment but in fact remaining firmly bound to the problem and developing patterns of obsessive behaviour to help them both conceal their anorexia and make a pretence of coping with their lives.

An historical perspective

Most of the ancient civilizations of which we have direct knowledge seem to have contained not only very definite ideas about what was good to eat[4] but also clear preferences as to the ideal shape of the human body. Some of the most primitive sculptures we have depict mother goddesses with huge bellies and enormous breasts. These come from the civilization which developed in the Indus valley, and like many peoples who lived in constant fear of famine and starvation these people seem to have prized fatness, particularly among women; it was evidence of a woman's fertility and of the likelihood that she would bear and nourish healthy children.

In certain African and Middle Eastern cultures today, to be fat is considered a sign of both health and affluence. In some Jewish communities, especially poor ones, fat children are assumed to be more healthy than thin ones, though, as we shall see, this is a view much out of keeping with Western social thought in general.

The ancient Greeks and Romans did not at all approve of obesity (at least, the affluent classes did not) and it seems that Roman women were expected to adhere to very rigid stereotypes of thinness, much as are the women of today. It is perhaps not surprising that the Romans, with their affluence and love of good food, invented the vomitorium, enabling themselves to dispose of their over-indulgence without putting on weight. This is reminiscent of the stories we hear today of groups of American college girls overeating together and then making themselves sick as a kind of collective activity.

In Elizabethan times, in spite of the well-documented excesses of the court, the Queen was said to have had a waist around which a man's two hands could meet. Whether one believes this or not, the pattern seems to be clear: wherever and whenever there has been a superabundance of food, thinness, the ability to abstain from it, has been socially valued. In societies in which food is a scarce resource, where there isn't enough to go round, then thinness is associated with poverty, ill-health and fear.

If we acknowledge that throughout history, at least among privileged classes, there have been clear social preferences for one body shape rather than another and that food has certainly contained meanings which transcend mere survival, we have to ask to what extent eating disorders are really a new phenomenon. We know for certain that anorexia nervosa has a history going back for over 100 years.

It was in 1874 that the symptoms of self-starvation were first given this name. Sir William Gull, an English physician, carefully documented his cases, and at about the same time a French doctor, Lasegue, reported something very similar. As early as 1689, Dr Richard Morton described a young woman with symptoms which he did not understand, but which to us can be nothing other than anorexia nervosa. Rudolph Bell, in his book *Holy Anorexia*,[5] puts forward the intriguing thesis that some of the medieval saints, with their feats of asceticism which were particularly concerned with abstinence from food, so resemble the present-day anorexic that one might be able to trace a thread of continuity.

One of the current authors[6] has also been impressed with the power of the ascetic tradition which seems so dominant in anorexia, and has suggested that guilt about sexuality and femininity may provide a link between the early 'desert mothers' and the anorexics of today. In all the major religious traditions (Christianity, Judaism, Islam, Buddhism) there has always been a strand of thought which encourages a split between mind (soul, spirit) and body.

Very often the body, with its physical demands – for food, sex and comfort – is depicted as an impediment to the spiritual fulfilment of the individual. To the anorexic of today, the body is very often perceived as something which 'gets in the way' of the 'real' person, who does not have such base and ordinary needs. It seems entirely likely, therefore, that although anorexia was carefully documented and named only 100 years ago, it has existed in a variety of forms within different cultures from the very beginning of civilization – in any culture, in fact, where food could be regarded as an indulgence rather than a necessity and where the spiritual aspect of humankind was conceived of as separate and distinct from the physical body.

Compulsive eating – which is a contemporary construction for describing an age-old dilemma – has without doubt been with us from earliest times. In religious terms it is often labelled as greed or gluttony, and it was regarded as one of the seven deadly sins. This kind of judgement, which remains with us today, is unfortunate, as many women today who eat to fulfil needs other than hunger are still encouraged to think of themselves as suffering from a form of moral weakness rather than as expressing a psychological, emotional difficulty through food.

We know little about the prevalence of bulimia in past societies. Undoubtedly some people have always made themselves sick to relieve the feeling of fullness following a heavy meal, but we do not know whether in the past it became the self-destructive obsession we so often see today. We do know, however, that women have been making themselves sick for at least the last twenty years; women are now coming forward for help in later life and telling us that their bulimia is a compulsive secret which they have hidden for nearly all of their adult lives.

Eating disorders today

There has probably never before been a time when so many women in the Western world find their lives dominated by food. It is not just teenagers, but women throughout their lives and into old age, who experience a continual struggle with and against food and their own desire and need for it.

Anorexia itself is still a relatively rare condition. Roger Slade[7] quotes figures of approximately 1 in 200 girls under sixteen at independent schools, with 1 in 100 over sixteen. It seems that at state schools the figure is considerably lower. Slade goes on to give the quite astounding figures of 1 in 50 university students overall, with 1 in 14 for dance schools and schools of modelling. We can see that anorexia is a highly selective disorder: 9 out of 10 anorexics are female, and they tend to be young and to be high achievers educationally. A 1981 study of what is known as 'sub-clinical' anorexia showed that approximately 5 per cent of post-pubertal females develop a form of anorexia which is probably too mild actually to require treatment.[8] In 1983 Clarke and Palmer[9] studied eating attitudes in university students and found that 11 per cent, although not anorexic, had attitudes comparable to anorexics.

Bulimia appears to be much more common. A survey of college students in the USA[10] revealed that 19 per cent of women and 5 per cent of men experienced all the major symptoms of bulimia. This is certainly a very high percentage of the college population. In our experience, however, bulimia is not limited to young women at college. Although some bulimics have previously suffered from anorexia, many more develop it in their twenties when they are already well established in careers and sometimes in marriages. It is impossible to determine the actual incidence of bulimia. It is a highly secretive symptom, and for all the women who come forward and ask for help we are probably right to infer that there are many more who do not.

As for compulsive eating, it is probably true to say that there are as many compulsive eaters as there are dieters; this means that at some time in their lives, most women will have had the experience of feeling out of control around food. For a substantial minority of women, dieting, and in consequence compulsive eating, become a way of life. Every day is a new challenge for such women, and failure to control their eating becomes each day a source of shame which further decreases their already low sense of self-esteem. In our experience, compulsive eaters are drawn from all social classes and walks of life. We see highly educated and successful women from privileged backgrounds whose lives are dominated by an obsession with food. We have also run compulsive eating groups in local women's centres where the group members were poor and occupying very traditional women's roles in relation to their families.

All the eating disorders – anorexia, bulimia and compulsive eating – unquestionably occur across all social classes and racial groups, in London at least. There is still a tendency for women who develop an acute anorexic disorder early in their lives to be doing very well educationally, though this does not necessarily mean that they are white and middle-class.[11] Some possible reasons for this will be discussed in Chapter 2.

There seems no question that the incidence of eating disorders has increased dramatically in the past twenty years. Older doctors, who were told during their medical training that anorexia was a rare condition they would hardly ever see, now complain that they see new cases every week. Bulimia was not recognized as a clinical entity until 1979; up until that time, the few cases that came to light were confused with and treated as anorexia. Now, whenever there is a television programme mentioning bulimia as a problem, a flood of new referrals come forward – often women who have concealed their secret obsession for years. Compulsive eating came out of the closet as a problem for women in 1978 with the publication of Susie Orbach's *Fat is a Feminist Issue*. At last someone had given a name to the problem which had tormented so many women for so long.

In attempting to understand the alarming increase in eating disorders in recent years, a number of writers have pointed to increasing social pressures on women to be slim. While it is certainly true that the ideal woman of today is considerably thinner than her counterpart in the 1950s, we probably need to look back to the Victorian era to understand the origins of the present epidemic of eating disorders. In the 1870s, women from the middle classes began in large numbers to develop a series of malaises, the symptoms including fainting, weakness and loss of appetite.[12] While some descriptions of these women sound very like present-day anorexia, others sound more like manifestations of depression. However, the one thing the descriptions have in common is that the woman was rendered weak, powerless and in a sense the heroic victim of her illness. It was a widely held cultural belief at the time that girls and women from wealthy families should be frail, weak and dependent, with little power or autonomy in their own right. Women's physical and mental constitution, it was believed, made them unsuitable for any kind of work or intellectual activity. The burdens of menstruation and, later, childbirth were thought to sap a woman's strength and render her capable of little else. It is interesting, though, that while Victorian doctors could write texts on the inherent weakness of women, they did not include in their thinking their own maids, or the thousands of women and girls who worked fourteen- and fifteen-hour days in the new industrial towns which created the wealth of the era. With this contradiction at the heart of their thinking, it comes as little surprise that well-off Victorian women and girls developed psychological illnesses in order to fulfil the roles demanded of them.

The resurgence of eating disorders in the 1960s also came at a time when women were facing a crisis in terms of their roles and their possibilities. By that time, many women were experiencing profound changes in their lives. The modern feminist movement was articulating new demands for women to take up a full and equal role alongside men; the major professions and educational opportunities were by this time open to women. Yet at another level, our thinking about women had not changed and it still has not. Our concept of femininity still contains within it the idea of weakness, dependence and self-denial. We shall see later on how women have internalized these ideas and how they unconsciously express their conflicts through their eating.

Although women's lives have changed a great deal, it is likely to take a long time for these internal perceptions to change. It is also important to understand that women alone cannot bring about changes in how they feel about themselves and about femininity. It is not just women themselves, but society in a more general sense, which prefers women to be somewhat powerless and childlike, and certainly to look like little girls.

Eating problems as metaphors

The dictionary defines a metaphor as 'the application of a name or descriptive term to an object to which it is not literally applicable'. In other words, a metaphor is something which symbolically, not literally, represents something else. Throughout this book we will be treating eating disorders as metaphors for another kind of reality, another level of difficulty for women.

Eating disorders are very often taken literally. In Chapter 8, we will look at the misconceived attempts to help women with eating disorders which result from taking them literally, from believing that the eating disorder *itself* is the problem rather than a metaphor or symbolic representation of it. Any treatment initiative which takes this narrow view will focus exclusively on trying to eradicate the disordered eating behaviour without understanding the underlying meanings and causes of it. At the other extreme, a traditional psychotherapeutic way of responding to eating disorders has sometimes been to ignore the symptoms completely and to try to understand the underlying problems without reference to them. Neither of these approaches can be complete without an attempt to understand and work from the meeting point of the symptom and the underlying problem. This meeting point is the metaphor, the symbolic representation of the woman's inner world via the eating problem. The behaviour around food is an overt but coded message which expresses but also hides the woman's emotional world. It is through the eating problem that we can learn about and understand her unconscious emotional world, her relationship to her own needs, to people close to her and to the world around her. It is not only the woman's eating behaviour which we need to consider, but also her body size, which is another aspect of her symptom.

Throughout the book we consider the symptom, which includes both the disordered eating behaviour and the woman's body size, together with an analysis of women's psychology in an attempt to see into her unconscious, conflictual inner world. As we continue, the meanings of eating disorders and the way in which they serve as metaphors for women's inner reality will become clearer. In a general way, we can understand eating disorders as signs that the woman has difficulties in the area of identifying her own needs and in allowing those needs to be met.

The need for food, the response to hunger, is the most basic and primitive need which human beings experience. In our earliest experiences of feeding, the meeting of our biological need for food and our emotional needs for care, love and nurturing come together. When a mother feeds her baby, she also holds the baby, comforts her and provides the sense of safety in which the baby can feel relaxed and secure and can grow and thrive. For all of us, at the beginning of our lives, feeding, taking in food, also stands for the taking in of emotional care and the meeting of our emotional needs.

Eating disorders symbolically represent disorders or difficulties in the area of emotional needs. This is generally true of all eating disorders, but if we look more carefully at the particular constellation of symptoms which each woman produces, we can learn more about the nature of those difficulties.

The compulsive eater, the woman who eats when she is not hungry and feels herself constantly preoccupied with her wish to eat and her simultaneous wish to resist food, is certainly aware of having needs. Indeed, she very often feels needy and empty as though she desperately wants something inside her. However, instead of allowing herself to be fully aware of what those needs really are, she reaches for food and submerges her needs, stuffs them down with food.

At the same time, she feels terribly guilty about her needs. She cannot perceive them and attempt to meet them in a straightforward way. Her needs are a source of shame, which is represented by her fat, which for her is a direct result of her being so needy.

The anorexic, on the other hand, seeks to live out her life in a way which denies all needs. She behaves as though she were self-sufficient. The message she attempts to communicate to the world is that she has no needs at all; she believes, or wants to believe, that she doesn't need relationships or anything at all from other people – she doesn't even need that most fundamental human necessity, food.

As we shall see later, the anorexic is terrified of her own needy feelings. Through her anorexia, she achieves a state of mind in which she is quite cut off from them and can really convince herself that she is not like other people. Unlike the compulsive eater, the woman who develops anorexia cannot tolerate any sign of her own weakness. She refuses to have a body which proclaims her human needs – her hunger and her sexuality.

The bulimic woman, through her symptom, is expressing her profound ambivalence towards her own needs. At one moment, she feels a sense of uncontrollable neediness. Like the compulsive eater, she does not allow herself really to enter into and identify what it is that she needs. She attempts to 'deal with' her emotional needs with food, and the violence and ferocity with which she eats gives us some indication of the strength of those needs and the desperation she feels to calm her disturbed feelings.

As soon as she has eaten, the bulimic woman feels a compulsion to get rid of the food and to free herself of any reminder of her awful and terrifying needs. It is as though the food inside her, her attempt to meet her own needs, feels bad and poisonous and has to be got rid of. The food represents to her her own weakness, her own insatiable need which she regards as weakness. By her cruel rejection of the food she has taken in, the bulimic woman manages to push away that part of herself which she experiences as needy, demanding and unacceptable. At the same time, she

What Are Eating Disorders?

controls her weight by her vomiting and thus removes from public view that part of her which she so despises. Unlike the compulsive eater, she does not have the fat on her body to say to the world, and to remind her, that she is a needy person, sometimes a distressed person – that all is not well.

Throughout this book, we will be exploring the different ways in which women express their distress through their food, the way they eat and their expression of themselves through their bodies. But more importantly perhaps, we will be pointing to the way forward for women. For each story we tell of the apparent hopelessness, loneliness and despair which can be engendered by these problems, there is another story of strength and determination. The more we have learned about the difficulties which women encounter in their lives, the more we have seen of the capacity of women to face and to overcome these problems.

All women, but particularly young women, are living through a time which is especially troubled and troubling – in an emotional sense, as well as the more obvious material and environmental ones. The struggles and difficulties which we describe here are indicative of distress and discomfort, sometimes protest, but also growth and potential change.

Eating disorders are very complex difficulties; generalizations are never entirely satisfactory, and in a book such as this we can do no more than scratch the surface of what such a problem will be about for any particular individual. However, and most importantly, eating disorders are meaningful difficulties. They are not impossible to understand, and understanding is the first step towards recovery.

Gone are the days when anorexia could be expected to run a crippling and chronic course, or when to be a compulsive eater meant a life sentence of obesity and unhappiness. Every year, we meet and work with women who overcome their eating disorders and find different and more effective ways of coping with their lives. It is our belief that if there were a more consistent and sympathetic understanding of the problems, this number would be much greater.

NOTES

1 A. H. Crisp, R. L. Palmer and R. S. Kalucy (1976): 'How Common is Anorexia Nervosa? A Prevalence Study', *British Journal of Psychiatry*, 128, 549–54.

2 S. Orbach (1978): *Fat is a Feminist Issue*, Hamlyn, London.

3 M. Dana and M. Lawrence (1988): *Women's Secret Disorder*, Grafton, London.

4 M. Harris (1986): *Good to Eat*, Allen & Unwin, London.

5 R. Bell (1985): *Holy Anorexia*, University of Chicago Press, Chicago and London.

6 M. Lawrence (1979): 'Anorexia Nervosa: The Control Paradox', *Women's Studies International Quarterly*, 2, 93–101.

7 R. Slade (1984): *The Anorexia Nervosa Reference Book*, Harper & Row, London.

8 E. J. Button and A. Whitehouse (1981): 'Subclinical Anorexia Nervosa', *Psychological Medicine*, 11, 509–16.

9 M. G. Clarke and R. L. Palmer (1983): 'Eating Attitudes and Neurotic Symptoms in University Students', *British Journal of Psychiatry*, 142, 299–304.

10 K. Halmi, J. Falk and E. Schwartz (1981): 'Binge Eating and Vomiting: A Survey of a College Population', *Psychological Medicine*, 11, 697–706.

11 M. Lawrence (1984): 'Education and Identity: Thoughts on the Social Origins of Anorexia', *Women's Studies International Forum*, 7, 4, 201–10.

12 B. Ehrenreich and D. English (1979): *For Her Own Good*, Pluto Press, London; J. Brumberg (1988): *Fasting Girls*, Harvard University Press, Cambridge, Mass.

2
ANOREXIA

For anyone who has never had first-hand experience of it, the words 'anorexia nervosa' can have a rather romantic ring. Psychiatry has distinguished the symptom with an intriguing Latin name, and it is often associated with glamorous young women – film stars, models, even royalty. It can conjure up images of beautiful, fragile, aesthetic creatures wasting away in spite of all the attempts of family and physicians to tempt them to eat.

Anyone who has suffered from anorexia, has seen the problem within their own family or has worked with anorexics will know how very false this romantic picture actually is. The name of the disorder itself is misleading. Anorexia nervosa literally means nervous loss of appetite. In fact, anorexics do not lose their appetites. Rather, appetite, like every other uncontrollable desire and feeling, is, at an unconscious level, viciously suppressed and denied.

As for glamour, this is another association which is misleading and unhelpful to our understanding of the problem. If we were to be flies on the wall at a meeting of the Eating Disorders Association, the charity which sets up and supports self-help groups in many towns and villages throughout the country, we should not find ourselves in the company of film stars or royalty. Instead, we would encounter several anxious, confused families, each containing a daughter, too frightened to speak, and a number of older women wearily trying to cope with the realities of what can feel like a crippling disability.

Anna, when she first entered therapy, also began to go to her local Anorexic Aid group with her parents. She was seventeen, very tall for her age and weighing no more than $6\frac{1}{2}$ stone. Anna was a clever girl, the eldest in a family of three girls, and was studying hard for her O-levels when things started to go wrong. She was a charming girl, gifted not only academically but at music and sport. Anna had no idea what had happened or what was happening to her. Her family had seen their loved and prized daughter change from a young woman in whom they had all their hopes to a secretive, irritable and despairing girl who dominated the family both with her bizarre demands around food and her seeming inability to make use of any of the care and concern they were holding out to her. She herself often felt troubled and upset when she was with her family. She didn't know why. She longed to be close to them, to tell them about herself, but was always lost for words and pushed them away.

The more weight Anna lost, the more anxious her mother became. They argued and shouted at each other. Anna wept, then denied there was a problem. She often felt ill and was constantly cold, and yet she continued to feel terrified of food and sometimes wished she could die. Her mother noticed the fixed, lifeless stare in Anna's eyes and the foul, acrid smell of her breath. Despite her secretiveness and reticence, Anna's mother had caught sight of the soft downy hair which now covered her daughter's body. In desperation she began to put high-calorie powder into the tiny amount of food her daughter would eat. Anna suspected. She refused to eat anything which she had not prepared on her own, while her mother was out. Mother was distraught. Father became angry. He had always left his wife to deal with his three daughters and had been content himself to stay in the background. Now it was decided he should take a firm hand with Anna. Within a few days, his relationship with Anna had almost completely broken down; he just could not understand her irrational refusal either to eat her mother's food or to talk about her problems. He wanted to be helpful, but eventually he found her silence and her withdrawal too much to manage. He began to stay later at work and almost to dread coming home to his wife's and daughter's tears.

Not a glamorous picture. But this is the reality of anorexia.

It is not always accomplished young women who suffer from anorexia. Stephanie was thirty-two years old when she first began to have problems with food. She had become very depressed after the birth of her first baby, Simon, and when she had Julia two years later she began to become preoccupied with her weight. Always a fairly robust size fourteen, Stephanie shrank rapidly to a size ten and was soon causing her husband and parents concern. She tried harder and harder to be a good mother, but secretly her major preoccupation was with her weight and body size. She looked after her family, caring and cooking for them, but herself ate less and less.

Stephanie had married at twenty-five. She had never particularly wanted a career for herself, though after an 'average' education she had secured a good job in a bank. Marriage, after a long engagement, had seemed like the answer. Stephanie never doubted that she would have children and spent the early years of her marriage preparing for what she assumed would be the fulfilment of her life. She had no way of understanding what was happening to her any more than did her husband. When she first came for therapy, Stephanie was in a quiet, contained despair. She felt like an automaton. Her adored children, the husband she thought she loved, were unreal to her. She tried her hardest, but her only real feelings were in relation to her weight. She weighed herself three times every day. If the dial showed that she had lost weight, she felt able to carry on, even able to laugh and enjoy life for a moment. If she had not lost weight, Stephanie would be thrown into a deep, withdrawn hell. She could not look at her children. Her only dealings with them would be mechanical. She would smile at her husband, ask him about his day and pray that he would not demand any emotional or physical intimacy. And all this towards the people she most loved in her life.

This is the reality of anorexia.

It is often thought that anorexia affects only young girls from the middle and upper classes. In our experience, it can occur at any age between seven and seventy. While the overwhelming majority of anorexics are women or girls, a large and possibly growing number of boys and men also suffer from the disorder. In terms of social class, it is now clear that anorexia has no favourites. There is a strong tendency for anorexics to be high achievers and to do well educationally, and this is one of the key factors to account for the alarming incidence of anorexia in young women from the Indian subcontinent living in the UK. Later in this chapter, we shall explore the question of why some people develop anorexia while others do not. But first we need to try to understand something about the experience of anorexia. It is such a dramatic problem, with its real meanings so well hidden and so different from the symptoms produced, that we can best approach it as we would the peeling of an onion. If we begin with the outside layer, if we are careful, we can uncover more and more of what the symptoms mean.

While anorexia is rightly thought of as an avoidance of food, it is evident from the most simple conversation with a woman in an anorexic phase that she is totally obsessed *with* food. Most of her thoughts centre around how much she has eaten, what she will consume for the rest of the day, how much exercise she will be able to fit in and whether it will be 'enough'. One of the women who consulted us actually counted every step that she took each day in addition to her rigorous exercise schedule. At the end of the day, she could then calculate her total calorie output. If it was less than the previous day, the situation would be rectified with a nocturnal run.

The anorexic woman has become obsessed with having less and less and doing more and more. She can achieve a sense of well-being and self-respect only if she has forced her body to go through an ever more self-denying regime. At the same time, she utterly rejects and denies any idea that there might be something wrong. She always says that she feels 'fine', that she is not tired, not hungry, not cold. Anyone who suggests that her bizarre patterns of life are anything but 'fine' is viewed with suspicion. She feels under siege and anyone who tries to tempt her from her tower is seen as the enemy, however well-meaning she senses they may be.

Anorexia nervosa is not just about losing weight. That is why the label 'slimmer's disease', much loved by the popular press, is such a cruel one. It is not the anorexic's aim to make herself more attractive, more beautiful, more acceptable in the struggle for sexual security. Her battle is with herself and her goal is control. No one is there to judge her 'success'. She is not under external pressure to lose more and more weight, to subject herself to her agonizing deprivation. All her pressures are internal. It is she herself who is determined to overcome the part of herself she hates, cannot bear and wants to eradicate.

The woman in an anorexic phase is herself unaware of all this. Often her inner persecutor is experienced as external. She will react to any chance remarks from others, which she invariably interprets as critical of her size. Even when she is very, very thin, she will still be expecting people to judge her as too large. For her, the whole issue seems to be about weight and size. She has no way of understanding what her obsession covers up.

What is it that brings about this state of affairs? What stops so many talented young people from being able to enjoy life, enjoy themselves and instead subject themselves to such torment? And why does it feel so absolutely essential and non-negotiable? The answer to this perplexing question lies in the anorexic's quest for moral perfection. It is not that she wants to lose more and more weight for fashion or cosmetic reasons. She feels, rather, that to allow herself to meet any of her ordinary human needs, including food, is a sign of her own weakness, an expression of her selfishness and moral failure.

In this sense, anorexia is no different from bulimia and compulsive eating; all eating disorders result from putting on to food and eating all that we regard as the 'bad' part of ourselves. Most of the people who develop the symptom of anorexia are by temperament very self-critical, with a strong perfectionist element. Under particular kinds of stress, when a crisis threatens, the person who has already learned to see food and eating as something which has intense moral connotations may well come to feel that a renunciation, a giving up of all but the barest necessities, is the only way forward. Thus anorexia, to the woman caught up in that experience, does not feel like being caught up in a life-threatening psychological difficulty. Anorexia seems, on the contrary, like a solution to her problems; a way of overcoming the person she doesn't want to be and freeing herself from the needs and feelings which she cannot tolerate.

When does anorexia occur?

Anorexia can occur at any time within the life cycle, between seven and seventy. It usually occurs when the individual is undergoing a period of personal change which she does not feel able to cope with and adapt to. Any life-event which challenges a person's sense of autonomy and independence, which leaves her feeling dependent and out of control, can precipitate an anorexic episode. Very often, what in fact happens is that such experiences evoke earlier feelings connected with separation and autonomy which were not resolved satisfactorily.

A large number of anorexic episodes occur in young women between the ages of fourteen and twenty. Other women develop the problem after marriage and the birth of children. Anorexia has also been reported in older women, around issues of ageing and retirement. All of these crucial times in women's lives bring up problems and demand adjustments in social role, particularly regarding autonomy and dependence and perhaps more importantly in terms of how women see and feel about themselves.

The young women who develop anorexia are very often doing well at school and seem destined for success in the world. Anorexia seems to be connected to the kind of crisis in identity which educational success can create for girls.[1] While for boys, educational success is likely to enhance their social standing, for girls it presents something of a contradiction. In our society, we encourage girls to work hard, to do well, to pursue qualifications and a career, while at the same time continuing to teach very small girls that marriage and motherhood are essential aspects of femininity. We have not yet ourselves resolved our contradictory feelings about what women really 'should' do in the world. While ever more opportunities are open to women, we still regard 'career' women or 'blue stockings' with scorn and suspicion. Young women are expected to be both successful people in the world and, at the same time, feminine, sexual and with all the caring and self-denying attitudes we associate with motherhood. This is a tall order, and it is a dilemma we rarely discuss with young people.

Many young anorexics when they begin to recover from their eating disorder can talk freely of how confused and terrified they felt, both at their own awakening sexuality and at the conflicting demands they felt upon themselves. Anorexia, or at least the continual preoccupation with weight reduction which it entails, effectively deadens these feelings so that all the real conflicts become unconscious and the individual attempts to resolve her difficulties using her own body. Often a period of emotional turmoil and depression precedes an episode of anorexia. Weight loss, and the feelings of euphoria and increased control which it brings, initially make the young woman feel better.

There is recent evidence to suggest that young women who have been brought up in the UK, but whose families come from the Indian subcontinent, are particularly vulnerable to eating disorders. These are likely to be young women who have a more than usual difficulty in resolving the conflicts of adolescence and young adulthood. They will experience not only the social conflicts around women's roles which are so deeply entrenched in our culture, but also pressures from the culture which their families have left behind. In order to be a Western woman, the Indian girl has to give up a great many of the cultural assumptions which come from her family's past. Many young people from the Indian subcontinent work hard and do well educationally. This, for young women, puts them in a position of enormous conflict. In order to achieve an acceptable identity in one area, another aspect of identity has to be either integrated or given up. This amounts to an enormous developmental task and it is no wonder that many young women feel unequal to it.

Anorexia as a denial of feelings

Rather than thinking of anorexia as a 'problem' in itself, it is more useful to see it as an attempted solution to a series of problems which feel overwhelming. Self-starvation and the relentless regime of physical deprivation which goes with it effectively anaesthetize the individual to all emotions. The body feels, but the emotions do not. In particular, the young women who are vulnerable to anorexia find it very hard to tolerate what they regard as 'bad' feelings. These in fact are no more than ordinary human feelings, such as anger, envy, vulnerability and neediness. Adolescence and young adulthood are times in our lives when we often have very strong feelings. We may begin to see our parents in a new and different light and to feel anger at what we now consider to be their shortcomings. Our own insecurities about ourselves as potential adults may arouse strong feelings of envy, and all the childhood conflicts within the family which may not have been properly resolved now reassert themselves with a new force. And yet the young anorexic is quite out of touch with all of this. All she can feel is an intense desire and longing to keep herself under control, to make her body exist on less and less, and terrible feelings of shame and guilt when she fails. A determination, in fact, not to feel her feelings. In quite an unconscious way, anorexia does actually express anger towards her family. Whether she lives with mother and father, or whether she has a family of her own, by rejecting food, by refusing to eat with them, she is giving her family a powerful message that she is different, set apart and cannot participate with them in meeting her own needs. For many mothers, living with an anorexic daughter is a bitter experience. The mother is only too well aware that by rejecting her food, her daughter symbolically rejects her and her love and nurturing.

It is often said that anorexia is, unconsciously, an attempt at regression, a way of trying to return to childhood and a rejection of womanhood. The physical effects of anorexia, and in particular the loss of menstrual periods, have tended to focus attention on the sexual aspects of this 'regression' so that anorexia is sometimes described simply as a means of avoiding sexuality and sexual maturity. It is certainly true that some women who enter into an anorexic phase are pleased by the loss of their periods and relieved that they no longer have sexual feelings. Perhaps more importantly than this, many anorexics show a real nostalgia for childhood, a longing to return to the relationships they had in the family as children. Often the past is seen through rose-coloured glasses, as though childhood was a time in which everyone had only good feelings for each other. Rather than understanding anorexia as an avoidance of sexuality, it seems more accurate to see it as a denial of all the feelings associated with growing up, changing and leaving the family. Any feelings which 'rock the boat', including sexual feelings, seem overwhelming and anorexia can be a powerful means of remaining cut off from them.

Family patterns underlying anorexia

A great deal has been written about the role and responsibilities of families in the development of anorexia. It has even been suggested that anorexia is a symptom not of an individual dilemma, but of a disordered family.[2] In our experience, it is extremely difficult to make generalizations about the kind of families from which anorexics come. The stereotype of the 'anorexic family' suggests that it is middle-class, materially secure, often with a rather distant father and a mother who is over-anxious and obsessively concerned with the welfare of her children. This, of course, is the stereotype of the middle-class family in Western culture. The vast majority of families in our society do not conform to this picture and neither do the majority of families who have an anorexic member. With the changing roles of both women and men, many mothers also have jobs outside the home. A large number of families have only one parent, usually a woman, and it is comparatively rare to find families where a man is the sole earner. We have worked with anorexic women who come from families with every conceivable set of social arrangements, from a wide variety of racial groups, right across the social class spectrum.

It is also not necessarily true that families with an anorexic member suffer a particularly high level of disturbance or stress prior to the onset of the anorexia. It is of course very difficult to be clear about this. Most families, after the eating disorder has developed, feel under great stress and may well adopt some disturbed patterns of behaviour in an attempt to deal with this. Anna's family, at the time they came under the scrutiny of the 'helping professions', felt themselves to be in the grip of something they simply could not understand. Anna's mother had resorted to subterfuge in order to try to feed her daughter, while her father had discovered an angry, unsympathetic part of himself which he had hardly known existed. It would, however, be a mistake to assume that the family was functioning in this disordered way before Anna became anorexic. In fact it is often difficult, once an eating disorder becomes established, for a family to remember what life was like before.

Having said that anorexia by no means always occurs in families with very severe problems and that it is in itself responsible for producing difficulties in families, we should nonetheless expect any symptom of the severity of anorexia to be linked to the early experiences of the individual and to the attitudes, particularly towards the self, which are learned and internalized from the family.

We have already discussed the way in which eating disorders can best be understood as expressions of the difficulty women have in articulating their needs and asking for those needs to be met. We would therefore expect someone who develops anorexia to have learned that having needs and expressing them is so dangerous and unacceptable that saying 'no' to everything seems the only solution. If we look at the mother–daughter relationship, which we will be describing in some detail in subsequent chapters, we can readily see that far from being unusual or pathological, it is in fact the norm for girls to be taught from an early age by their mothers that their own needs are a source of conflict and should be kept rigidly under control. One of the anorexic's central concerns is that if she begins to allow herself to eat, her appetite will be insatiable. This fear is an expression of the way she feels she must control her emotional needs lest they completely overwhelm her.

Stephanie came from a 'good' working-class family. The eldest of four children, she had from an early age helped and supported her own mother, who worked hard outside the home in order that her children should have the best the family could manage. Stephanie had a deep sense of never having had enough of her mother's time and care, although her closeness to her mother enabled her to be largely unaware of these feelings. Much of her own neediness was expressed through her concern to meet her mother's needs. When she met her husband, Stephanie established a relationship similar in many ways to the one she had with her mother. She took a lot of responsibility in the relationship and made few demands. She enjoyed setting up a home and took pleasure in taking care of it and of her husband. It was when her first baby was born that Stephanie's unconscious feelings began to be stirred up. She identified with the needy baby and began to be aware of the needy baby inside herself. After a long period of anxiety and depression in the face of these feelings, she once again managed to bury them and carry on. With the birth of a daughter, with whom she had an even closer identification, Stephanie sensed that her own neediness was becoming uncontrollable. She had no idea of what it was she felt she needed and no belief at all that it was safe to explore such feelings. Instead, she began to try to cut off from them, using the symbolic medium of food. Limiting her food intake and taking rigid control of her body gave Stephanie a sense of well-being, a feeling that things were not, after all, out of hand. It was of course very easy for Stephanie to choose food to express her difficulties. Like many mothers with new babies, she was concerned about her figure and was encouraged to lose any extra weight remaining after the pregnancy.

We can see clearly here how the social preoccupations with women's bodies and with thinness come together with the psychological situation of many women in which they feel frightened and confused by their own emotional needs. Stephanie was very angry. Taking care of her needy dependent baby made her feel furious that she herself was so deprived. But such anger is terrifying. There she was, doing what she had been preparing all her life to do and feeling bitter and resentful towards the baby and the adults in her life she knew most loved her. Her tremendous guilt made her turn her anger against herself and punish her own body in the cruellest way. At the same time, she continued to go through the motions of being a 'good' wife and mother, thus expressing towards others the caring she craved for herself. Very little of all this was conscious to Stephanie. Her preoccupation with losing weight centred all her feelings on herself, so that she was largely anaesthetized to her 'bad' feelings towards others.

The vicious circle of anorexia

Anorexia occurs in women who have already developed a difficulty about tolerating and expressing the dependent, needy, childlike part of themselves. It can occur at any time when these needs are stimulated. For Anna, this was a time when she was reaching a stage when she should have been becoming more independent, less involved with her family and more prepared to think about herself as a person in the world. The conflicts which this produced made Anna feel like a little girl, wanting to scream at her parents that she was not ready for all this. As a 'good', undemanding girl, Anna was unable to tolerate these feelings and instead renounced all her neediness, symbolically, through her anorexia.

Once control of food intake and weight has been adopted, unconsciously, as a solution, certain gains occur which tend to reinforce it. First, the woman may initially find that her weight loss is admired. Friends and family make favourable comments, which encourages her to continue and confirms that she is doing the right thing. Secondly, she herself feels that she is in control of things. Weight loss, the dropping dial on the scales, is a tangible proof to her that she can by using her willpower overcome both her body and her feelings. In addition, fasting can itself produce a feeling of euphoria. The well-known 'fasting high' is a physiological consequence of reduced food intake, and it serves well to mask and transform feelings of depression and loneliness.

Once anorexia is established, all other problems seem to disappear, at least as far as the woman herself is concerned. The anorexic really has no thoughts for anything but how much food she has eaten, what she weighs and what she will eat next. All her feelings are experienced in relation to food. She will no longer experience envious feelings towards a sister who she believes claims too much of mother's attention; instead, she will become obsessively concerned with how much that sister eats, and whether it is more or less than herself. She no longer feels anger when her mother hasn't enough time for her. Instead she is filled with guilt if she allows herself to have even a mouthful more than her tiny allocation of food. Everything is turned around. She no longer feels deprived, but instead perceives herself as decadent, greedy and always in danger of having too much.

But of course, the needy feelings don't really go away. Women in an anorexic phase do feel hungry, but instead of taking hunger pangs as a sign of need, for the anorexic they reassure her that she has not had too much. She needs continual reassurance, and so of course she can never consider herself to be thin enough. If she allows her weight to stabilize, she will once again become aware of her feelings, the needy feelings which are always there below the surface. This in a sense is why the anorexic always feels that she is too fat, no matter how thin her body really is. When she says she feels fat, sees herself as fat, she is responding to her unconscious and to the knowledge that in spite of all her efforts to suppress them, she is full of needy feelings, of wishes to demand and devour all the caring and attention which consciously she rejects.

Both Anna and Stephanie did recover from their anorexic episodes, though for both it was an up-hill struggle.

Anna was eventually referred by her general practitioner to a therapist with experience of working with young people. In addition to her weekly individual therapy, Anna also had a number of joint sessions with her therapist and her family. This was a very painful time for them all. Anna's parents needed a great deal of courage to face up to their own and their daughter's hurt and angry feelings. Anorexia is the kind of problem which makes everyone, including the sufferer herself, feel desperately guilty. These feelings have to be lived through and lived with, but as Anna's father said, about six months into her treatment: 'We have some very stormy times at home and we all get upset from time to time. But now at least it seems to be about other things than just food; I can cope with upsets much better if I know what the upset is about.'

It was three years before Anna was sufficiently recovered to resume her studies, and probably another two years before she herself felt that she was really 'over' anorexia. At the time of writing, she is married with a son of fourteen months.

Anna was fortunate in having a family who were prepared to

help and support her recovery, even when this meant facing up to some uncomfortable truths about themselves. Stephanie was not so lucky. Although her husband was initially sympathetic, he soon became exasperated and finally came to believe that he had a wife who was chronically ill. Her mother was very critical of Stephanie, especially of her ability to care for the children. She did actually provide some valuable practical help with child care, but always in such a way as to make Stephanie feel undermined. She too seemed very ready to accept that her daughter would never recover.

In her therapy, Stephanie gradually came to feel more separate from her mother, less dependent on her and more able to withstand her criticism. Her marriage did not survive her recovery. Her husband met and later married a woman who was in fact disabled. Stephanie is bringing up her two children on her own. She finds it a struggle and often feels depressed. But she is no longer anorexic.

NOTES

1 M. Lawrence (1984): 'Education and Identity: Thoughts on the Social Origins of Anorexia', *Women's Studies International Forum*, 7, 4, 201–10.

2 S. Minuchin, B. L. Rosman and L. Baker (1978): *Psychosomatic Families: Anorexia Nervosa in Context*, Harvard University Press, Cambridge, Mass.

For a fuller discussion of the issues involved in anorexia, see M. Lawrence (1984): *The Anorexic Experience*, The Women's Press, London.

3

COMPULSIVE EATING

A compulsive eater is someone, usually a woman, who eats more than she needs or wants to, not in response to signs from her stomach indicating hunger but for quite different reasons. For the compulsive eater, physical and emotional cues become confused. She senses a need within herself, but then interprets it as a physical rather than an emotional sensation. Stomach hunger is an experience she does not allow herself to feel very often. She usually eats before this experience ever comes about. At times feeling hungry is quite frightening for her, and generally even detecting signs of physical hunger is a difficult task and becomes confused with other sensations and feelings. After years of eating without reference to physical hunger, the actual interpretation of signs of bodily hunger to the understanding 'I am hungry' is difficult in itself. There are two aspects to this difficulty of interpretation: she cannot recognize physical signs of hunger, and many emotional states such as discomfort, loneliness and anger are interpreted as hunger for food.

For the compulsive eater, most uncomfortable situations, whether physical or emotional, will immediately be interpreted as hunger for food and will be dealt with automatically by the pushing of something into her mouth. 'This morning I woke up, remembered last night's party and how awful I felt. I was still full from the huge amounts of food I consumed yesterday, but felt bad both emotionally and physically, so I had a huge breakfast. I felt so heavy that I didn't want to move, but I had to go to work. I hate my job. As soon as I arrived I had coffee and two cakes.'

Marie invited some friends for dinner. They were all couples and she felt she was the only unhappy one – she was the only one without a partner. After they had gone she felt very lonely, left on her own in the house. The party had ended and she was left to do the clearing up. There were tears in her eyes as she took the dishes to the kitchen; and suddenly, she found herself frantically eating all the leftovers from dinner. As she ate, she imagined her friends having what she really wanted: the emotional nourishment that comes from being with someone and feeling loved.

Marie's feeling of isolation and aloneness brings about a sense of sad longing, a need that she does not know how to meet. The term 'found herself' is important, as she often feels as though she is doing something out of her control, as if it is not really her but someone else who is doing the eating and she is merely an onlooker who desperately wants to stop what is happening and is unable to do so.

The compulsive eater is not necessarily overweight, since she may control her weight by fierce dieting between binges or by taking large amounts of laxatives, but in many cases the eating correlates with being or feeling overweight, having a very low self-image centred and concentrated on her body size, and feeling that her social identity and self-concept are solely determined by being overweight.

Many compulsive eaters are much more distressed about their size than their level of overweight actually justifies. A woman may feel herself to be 'huge', even though to other people she is only a little overweight. For her, her fat colours every aspect of her personality. The fat itself also serves as a bin into which disowned or disliked aspects of herself are discarded. Everything she does not like about herself, everything she does wrong, everything which goes wrong is blamed on her fat.

Elizabeth was fat. It was the reason, she believed, that she did not have a lover; because of being fat she was slow, did not have a sense of humour, was stupid. When something went wrong in her life, when for example she was not invited to a party that all her friends got invited to, she put this down to being fat. In short, all that she disliked about herself was related to if not caused by her body size.

The compulsive eater may go out with friends to a restaurant and, once there, will either eat a big meal with the others or deprive herself by eating very small quantities. If she eats, she feels guilty. If she doesn't, she feels deprived and frustrated. Either of these feelings may result in her returning home and raiding the kitchen. In these raids, or binges as they are called, she will not select what she takes in but will eat anything that comes to hand. Often she will just stand in front of the fridge and grab whatever is in sight. As one woman said: 'I realized I was looking in the fridge for feelings, only feelings do not live in fridges.'

Fighting Food

The woman eats and then wonders: 'How is it that I have just eaten half the food in the kitchen, and I still feel this all-consuming hunger that is still burning inside, no matter what I do or where I turn?' Obviously, in this non-selective hunger, there is not usually any discrimination involved. It is difficult to taste the food when you haven't chosen it or to experience it as nourishing when you feel so guilty about eating it. The compulsive eater eats constantly, as though to put out the small fires which keep igniting inside her and to prevent the violent uncontrollable explosion she so fears.

The feelings that are bound to follow are those of being out of control – of guilt, anger, weakness – and sure enough she falls back into self-disgust and self-hatred for being overweight and having eaten greedily yet again. Then comes the fantasy about tomorrow's diet, tomorrow's ideal size, when the thin beautiful woman inside her will bloom and flourish, when she will shrink to size such and such – and *then* her success story will begin, her real life will come to being.

But of course tomorrow never comes, or else it comes and goes again, and the fantasized wonderful kingdom of slimness remains *almost* within reach, and 'almost' and 'if only' become key words for the postponed life – put off to some point in the future when she will be thin and beautiful, all her problems solved.

Thoughts about food and eating or actual eating constantly occupy the compulsive eater. She is obsessed with food, addicted to it. The process that exists in all obsessions – the repetition of a thought or an activity in order to defuse a tension or solve an underlying conflict – expresses itself in the following way: 'I am worried, I feel tense, uncomfortable, therefore I eat, therefore I feel fat, therefore I no longer worry about the initial tension, rather I worry that I am fatter now. Now I am anxious about being fat – so – I eat again . . .' and so on. The cycle goes round, the guilt increases, and the cycle becomes tighter and tighter.

If she buys sweets, she feels guilty.

If she eats in a public place, she feels others are watching and judging her.

When eating in social situations, she is quite often embarrassed to show eagerness about food, and ashamed even to admit to liking food.

She eats her children's leftovers.

She thinks today about next week's dinner party, and while eating breakfast she is planning dinner.

She is the one at a buffet party who, if she manages to get to the table and fill her plate up, feels the need to apologize: 'I haven't eaten a thing all day.'

She will not usually think of what she *fancies* eating but rather what she *should* eat, or what is available. Little or no effort at all goes into finding out what she likes or dislikes, what she wants to eat at a specific moment.

Often she will not know what she really likes to eat. She has a list of what is forbidden and hence attractive, so her likes and dislikes are defined by what is allowed or forbidden. As one woman told us: 'For many years while I was dieting I thought my favourite food was chips because it was top of the list of forbidden foods, together with chocolate. Since I stopped dieting and feel I am allowed to eat both, I actually discovered that they were only so attractive to me because I was not allowed to eat them. Now I know I like them but they are not my absolute favourite.'

The woman who eats compulsively very rarely has a sensation of fullness, a sense of having had enough. This is because she is wanting not a physical sensation, but a feeling of emotional satisfaction. It was an emotional need which originally drove her to food, but as food cannot in fact satisfy that need, she never feels as though she has had enough.

'She' is one of a very high percentage of the women in Western society today who are either overweight or who feel themselves to be.

'She' is me, you, your next-door neighbour. She has no age limits, no specific class background, status or profession.

The 'common sense' approach to compulsive eating which some medical approaches endorse considers these women greedy, weak, and lacking in will-power and self-discipline. They are at times considered as women who do not care about their appearance, about themselves, who are neglecting themselves. If they cared about themselves, or had a bit of will-power, they would 'do something about it'.

If a woman is fat she is no competition to other women. They may consider her good-hearted, intelligent, lively, but at the same time she is not a threatening person to bring into the company of a lover or potential lover. While her friends may like her company, they subtly undermine her as a woman.

These are the sort of attitudes compulsive eaters have to contend with in their day-to-day existence. But if we really try to understand what compulsive eating is for women, greed, lack of self-discipline and will-power become nonsensical and inadequate explanations for a problem which needs understanding and compassion to get to its roots.

Who are these weak-willed women? They are women who in every area of their lives are full of will-power, discipline, initiative and strength; women who manage their lives in every detail with power and assertion; women who run houses with several children, cooking, cleaning, managing every single aspect of other people's lives as well as their own; women who manage offices; women who own and run businesses, who manage universities and who are powerful in many areas of life. These same women, when it comes to the area of eating, cannot find this amazing 'will-power' and 'discipline' they so amply possess in their work.

Fat is a Feminist Issue[1] was the first book which opened the way to seeing compulsive eating in a social context, as an adaptive mode of being, an attempt to cope with the world in which the woman lives and her conflicting feelings about her role in it. Susie Orbach wrote that 'being fat is a definite and purposeful act ... a directed conscious or unconscious challenge to sex role stereotyping and culturally defined experience of womanhood ... fat is *not* about lack of self-control or lack of will-power. Fat *is* about protection, sex, nurturance, strength, boundaries, mothering, substance, assertion and rage.' We will present here in brief some of the ideas that *Fat is a Feminist Issue* pioneered.

Compulsive eating has an apparent function of protection for the woman. Consciously or unconsciously this is how she perceives it. This is connected with women's role in society as second-class citizens, as providers of food and as people whose primary role is to meet the needs of others. Very often, a woman's attitude to food and to her own body as well as to her role in the world reflects and stems from her relationship with her mother.

The conflicts that arise from these issues are likely to be expressed by both eating compulsively and being 'overweight'. One example of this is the woman whose mother was always very concerned about her own figure. The woman has found a way of saying to her mother 'I do not want to be like you' through becoming overweight. This woman is likely to eat compulsively every time she has any contact with her mother.

The same eating pattern occurred in a woman whose mother was fat: in turn she became overweight, feeling sorry for her mother. Not wanting to compete and be better than her mother, she found a way to say this by being fat as well. Her statement was: 'I cannot bear to see you so miserable, alone and suffering, I will be like you and not threaten you with my distance and difference from you.' She and her mother would often eat large meals together.

But if we try to understand it more deeply, we can see that in reality the woman's fat was not necessarily a comfort to her mother and that probably she could have expressed her closeness and loyalty in other ways. For her, however (consciously or unconsciously), this was the only way she knew to express these feelings.

Susie Orbach's ideas, described in *Fat is a Feminist Issue*, were in their time – 1976 – radically new for a number of reasons. They not only took into account individual women's struggle with their eating, but presented a very realistic if pessimistic picture of most women in Western society as having some problems around food, eating and body-image. These problems were linked with the social situation of women in a patriarchal society. The struggle, though it is individual and personal, must be understood within a social context. There is a need to provide a collective explanation of why women have to face these struggles because of being women.

Another important idea in *Fat is a Feminist Issue* is that the woman's internal perceptions of her own weight and size are more important in understanding her problem than any external criteria. Thus it is the woman's sense of her own body which is taken into account, not whether or not she is under or overweight according to someone else's judgement. Connected with this is the fact that Orbach insists on calling compulsive eating a problem not an illness, disorder, disease or any term which tends to pathologize it.

It is the woman's experience which constitutes her struggle. It is her own definition which makes it a problem and it is not something she 'gets' or catches from somewhere but an expression of conflicts she experiences on both personal and social levels. By moving away from external to internal definitions of the problem, this approach also refrains from using any of the usual external criteria for defining weight, food and size, such as number of calories, amount of food consumption, 'good food and bad food', meal times, intervals between meals and 'normal' weight. It is the woman's own criteria (which are often determined by media 'dictates' and need to be worked with to become her own) that are the centre of the approach which in terms of 'treatment' has far-reaching implications: no one can do it for her, no one can dictate what her right size, weight is, and in the same way, no one can 'cure' her of her compulsive behaviour. It is hers, and her effort and understanding which will lead her to having control over her eating, her body size and her weight. This approach also puts the problem where it belongs, i.e. in the underlying conflicts and emotions which cause the compulsion and the obsessive thoughts about weight, size and food rather than in the symptom which is the weight itself.

While other approaches begin with an external definition of 'normal weight', the 'solution' will also be externally defined and controlled and the weight becomes the focus of both problem and solution. Diets become therefore a way of dealing with the symptom. The goal is the achievement of a certain 'normal' weight, again defined by medical charts related to height which do not take into account shape, bone structure or any other physical factors.

It is a well-known fact that 95 per cent of women who have dieted 'successfully' have put back the same or more weight than they have lost. There is ample research now to indicate that dieting actually makes the body more susceptible to putting on weight when the dieting stops.

If we look at the idea of dieting, it is a reduction in food intake, in calorie intake, in order to lose weight. The foods most desired by most dieters, such as chocolate, cakes, chips, etc., are the ones most prohibited by diet sheets. This idea of dieting, then, creates two problems. First the dieter begins to be obsessed with calorie-counting, good food and forbidden food, which makes food much more of an obsession than it already is. Hence the obsession increases, and with it of course a further avoidance of the real issues underlying the obsession. The second problem is that of deprivation. Often we hear women say, 'So I went on a diet, I lost weight, but am I going to be on a diet for the rest of my life? What about all these wonderful foods I love so much? Am I never going to be able to eat ice cream or chocolate?' Seeing other people enjoying their food is a painful experience for a dieter; they seem able to eat all they want and have no problem about how much or what they eat. As for the dieter herself, she needs to calculate, think, consider every mouthful. The world of food and restaurants becomes a source of constant agonizing debate with herself on what, how much, how little, she can allow herself to eat. The world itself can seem like a source of deprivation.

It has become very clear from working with many women in individual and group therapy that it is a sense of deprivation that causes the initial urge to eat when not hungry. This deprivation may be experienced in relation to the good things in life that others seem so capable of having and enjoying, such as love, fun, relationships, excitement and so on. As we shall see in later chapters, these feelings are rooted in early life, but here we are talking about the feeling which is highlighted by a sense of being an outsider because of being 'fat'. This is one of the ways of being deprived of the good things in life. The idea of diet as double deprivation then becomes very clear: the reason for turning to food in the first place is a feeling of lack, need, deprivation, something missing, and the inability to enjoy the kind of food that the dieter likes and *desires* increases that sense of not being part of the world of people, of not deserving the enjoyment and excitement of relationships and all the other good things that life offers, even simple accessible ones such as food. The sense of deprivation then leads to a much greater urge for these desirable/forbidden foods and a vicious circle of dieting following by bingeing, followed by another diet and then a binge. It is a very familiar pattern for many women that embarking on a new diet is preceded by a night of serious uncontrollable bingeing. 'If I start tomorrow and am really going to lose all that weight – I might as well make the best of it tonight, as there may not be another chance for a long time.' It is also a familiar pattern that after the end of a strict diet a woman may still keep some restrictions on her food intake for a day or two, and then the bingeing will start.

Abraham and Llewelyn Jones's study[2] of a group of 106 women students shows that 94 per cent had dieted at some time, the majority first doing so between the ages of thirteen and eighteen.

In a recent English study, Wardle[3] found that 75 per cent of a group of 161 schoolgirls between the ages of twelve and eighteen restricted what they ate (half of them nearly all the time) in an attempt to control their weight. The corresponding figures for boys were 39 per cent and 13 per cent (total 186). These figures are obviously very alarming, for a number of reasons – the number of women or girls who engage in restricting their food intake, the intensity of that restriction, and the early ages at which girls are beginning to be aware of their weight and the need to manipulate their figures. At as early an age as seven, girls learn that their appetites should not exceed ladylike limits and that their figures should not be spoilt by undesirable fat.

This is one of the exercises we use in self-help groups and study days to help people understand and feel the pain and harm involved in the idea of dieting: we ask each person in the group to think about an activity he or she does on a daily basis and which he or she feels to be vital for their well-being, something which is pleasurable and which means a lot to them in terms of leisure (like talking to a friend, playing the piano, having a bath). We ask them to luxuriate in fantasizing about it, all the wonderful feelings it brings, and what it means in their lives. We then say to them: we now give you an order to abolish this activity completely out of your life. You must never ever do it. You cannot lie and do it in secret because we will know, you will be severely punished, even if no one sees you when you actually do it, it will show on you and we will know. You are going to be ostracized and stigmatized as a *bad* person. We go on emphasizing the bad nature of this pleasurable thing, how forbidden it is to do it and the consequences of 'cheating'. The reactions range from violent fantasies about hitting and killing us, through rebelliousness, anger and hate, to despairing acceptance and pained misery about having to give it up.

It is helpful to think about a diet in this way, as it really opens one's eyes to the cruel, painful and humiliating aspects of dieting as well as to the rebelliousness and anger which diets can engender.

The meaning of compulsive eating – a case history

Esther was very skinny until she was fifteen, when she started putting on weight excessively. Her weight fluctuated throughout her teens, and she was put on a diet which resulted in a cycle of bingeing and dieting for many years. Some events in her life – leaving home and moving to another country, for example – brought loneliness, misery and with them massive overeating episodes and weight gain. Other events like falling in love and being rejected brought with them a loss of appetite and of weight. In Esther's words: 'But, of course, a few months later it all started again. I went on a diet, then a binge, then a diet, then a binge. I had an annual cycle – in the summer I would be thin and in winter fat.'

Years of losing weight and gaining it, dieting and bingeing, eventually resulted in a fat figure that Esther felt she could do nothing about. Her obsession with her looks was constant: she was preoccupied with her appearance, weighing herself constantly, always knowing somewhere inside herself that she was going to put back any weight she lost. She read *Fat is a Feminist Issue*, and joined a compulsive eating group. She felt that the most important thing she got from the group was the permission to eat foods she never allowed herself, or only binged on.

Another important discovery for Esther was why she was eating obsessively – that there was a reason. She describes it: 'I was living with a family at the time and I was afraid that the wife would think that I wanted her husband. Immediately I remembered that when my mother came for a visit, I went to meet her at the airport in my worst clothes, dirty, I didn't wash my hair for two weeks, looked horrible and ate like crazy. And the day she left I put on new nice clothes and had my hair done. So it came to my mind suddenly that I was opting out of any competition, especially in a situation with a couple.'

When trying to think about how the obsession had begun, and the events in her life at the time which led to her problems with food and eating (she says she was not familiar with the term compulsive eating), Esther says: 'People are fat and people are thin. People who are fat are those who eat a lot. But it never occurred to me to stop and think whether I was hungry or to question my eating patterns. I can't even remember the way I was eating. My father used to make sandwiches for me to take to work, I used to eat them at night, and put the bag (looking full) in the fridge. One night my mother caught me. I was in the kitchen. I was eating and she came in. I rushed to the balcony to hide. She came after me. "What are you doing there?" she asked. "Don't come in," I shouted at her. She tried to open the door. I tried to hold it shut. My mouth was full of food (this was 2 o'clock in the morning, when I had just come back from my boyfriend's). "Please don't come in," I begged. Then she pushed the door and saw me eating. She said, "I thought you had been raped. My God, you are stealing food from yourself." I can always relate it to feeling rejected by men.'

In therapy Esther got in touch with a tremendous hunger. She felt she was like a bottomless pit, as if she had a hole in her stomach. At her therapy sessions she wanted to talk only about food. An important aspect of her compulsive eating was her sexuality. For a long time she had no relationships, and when eventually she did, she started to eat compulsively again. She was happy, but was eating carelessly. 'I remember one night, we had dinner and were going to bed. As I went upstairs to brush my teeth I went into the kitchen and ate the leftovers – things I didn't even like. I wasn't even enjoying it. I went to bed, and with this image of these tomatoes in my stomach – I couldn't even make love to him. I thought: "How can I make love with these tomatoes in my stomach?" And I didn't want him to touch me or look at me. How can he want me? I thought. How can he like me? There was something really peculiar about it – this man really loved me. He put me on a pedestal. I wanted to have a fault, so I wanted to become fat. The idea was: "He doesn't want me because I am fat." I wanted to be sexually unattractive. I had to put up a barrier. Also, I wanted to make him feel better about himself. He had problems too.'

For Esther, compulsive eating was both a way to protect herself from the care, the love, the intimacy which were so frightening, and a way to protect her partner. This way they did not have to feel or talk about the real fear, the real problems – there were the compulsive eating and the fat to be obsessed with instead. She describes how with women she always felt in competition. The only women she could feel at ease with were fat women. The best way for her to opt out of competition at that time was to become fat and to be with fat women.

Esther describes how things began to change: 'Two things strike me – when I started to mother myself, to really take care of myself in a very nice and caring way, I didn't need to eat so much. I was always led to believe that I needed to have a boyfriend in order to be happy. And then I realized I could mother myself, take care of myself in other ways rather than food. When I didn't have a man I started to buy records, books, and other nice things for myself. I didn't necessarily have to have a man around to be nice to myself. That was really a turning-point in my life. I was really kind to myself in the nicest way ever for the first time in my life. I stopped treating myself through food.'

Esther felt she had to mother the men she had relationships with, but when she mothered them she didn't want to be sexual with them. She could be either a mother or a sexual partner – as if she was saying: 'You can't have me both ways – you can't have me mother you and have sex with me as well.' She realized that, like many compulsive eaters, she did not allow herself to have orgasms. The feeling that no one would have the patience to wait for her, that she could never have enough when she needed it, was equally present in relation to both sex and food: 'Grab while you can; food is timeless, spaceless and does not need partners to wait or to be patient with you. It is always there.'

Esther felt herself to be empty, unseen and unnoticeable. She attempted to counter this feeling by always filling herself up, making herself big and noticeable (at the same time, paradoxically, hiding herself inside the fat). She felt constantly out of control: it was as though she had two people inside herself – 'a complete split between the one who is eating and the one who is hating and despairing'. She says: 'I could not enjoy eating, could not enjoy visiting friends, not enjoy holidays. I couldn't enjoy anything because anywhere you go you have to meet your enemy. It's real suffering. My mother used to say: "Dieting is the most difficult and the most easy thing in the world to do."'

Esther's story illustrates many of the important issues involved in compulsive eating. Her account of her life is especially useful; she has been in therapy and in a self-help group, so therefore has some understanding of her own behaviour and of her relationship with herself and others.

Building on the understanding of compulsive eating set out in *Fat is a Feminist Issue*, the Women's Therapy Centre has had many years experience of working with women like Esther and has developed a distinctive approach. It may be helpful if we set out some of the basic assumptions of this approach:

Fighting Food

- The emphasis is on a woman's feeling about herself.
- Compulsive eating is merely a symptom, not the problem in itself.
- Weight is not the main issue.
- Compulsive eating is related to women's situation in society.
- There is a need to challenge society's ideas about women's size and shape.
- Getting fat can be an attempt to make such a challenge.
- Getting or feeling fat or overweight is a way of making a statement.
- Getting or feeling fat can have a protective function for women.
- Women take care of others through food but see it as an enemy to themselves.
- Women's lives are often controlled and dictated by activities which are done for others – husband, children, boss, parents.

Esther's underlying needs were all 'met' by eating compulsively. For example, when she visited a friend and wanted to talk about her desperation, the friend spent the whole evening talking about her own problems instead of listening to her. Esther, finding that her need to be listened to was not met, ate a whole cream cake in front of her friend – showing her friend graphically that she was in need, but was not able to say so. When she needed company, she would go to the cupboard. When she needed warmth, she went to the refrigerator – these are always cold, however, and do not give out warmth on demand. Whenever she was unable to ask for what she wanted or needed, she would eat instead; as she says: 'Food is always there – no need for appointments or asking or disappointments. Whatever you need, food is always there for you.'

The contradiction became obvious when Esther started taking care of herself and giving herself good things, not just eating. She allowed herself books, records and relationships with others. When she went to a restaurant, wanting to 'treat' herself in the old way, she found she was not hungry and realized she was no longer a compulsive eater. Food as such was not a treat any more, and gratification could come only from a real answering of her needs.

Esther expresses many important ideas about sexuality and intimacy. She uses fat as a barrier, a protection from sexuality and intimacy as well as an excuse for not having them. Throughout her story we hear echoes of her feeling of being horrible, of despair, self-hatred, emptiness and the constant attempt to shut these feelings off through eating compulsively and being obsessed with food. Her story is a good example of how compulsive eating serves a variety of functions in relation both to food and eating and to being fat. It is also an important illustration of how, as a woman becomes more painfully in touch with her real needs and feelings, compulsive eating can be given up.

NOTES

1 S. Orbach (1978): *Fat is a Feminist Issue*, Hamlyn, London.

2 Cited in G. Parry-Crooke and J. Ryan (1986): *Evaluation of Self Help Groups for Women with Compulsive Eating Problems*, Health Education Authority, London.

3 ibid.

4
BULIMIA

Overeating and then being sick is a comparatively common piece of behaviour among women who are concerned about their weight. Many women who diet rigorously sometimes resort to this practice if they break their diets. It has been reported that on American campuses the practice is widespread, and that young women often overeat and vomit with groups of friends and regard this almost as a form of recreation. There is in fact a broad continuum in terms of how seriously one should take the problem.

At one end is the dieter who may very occasionally make herself sick. At the other is the woman whose life is dominated by her bulimia and who may make herself sick ten or fifteen times a day, leaving her time and energy for very little else. While it may be a matter for regret that women should ever have to resort to such a self-destructive means of controlling their weight, it must be conceded that for some women, occasionally making themselves sick may not constitute a very serious problem. At the other, more serious end of the continuum, bulimia is not merely an aid to slimming. One of the blocks to understanding it fully has been the tendency to regard it as such.

While many women first 'discover' bulimia in an attempt to control their weight, those who get 'hooked' on the symptom are using it to solve much more serious problems. In its serious and addictive form, the vomiting is not merely a way of dealing with having overeaten. One could equally say that women overeat in order to make themselves sick. The symptom has to be seen as a whole. It is the taking in and throwing out of food which provides the key to its meaning.

Bulimia is a problem which arouses intense feelings in the people who try to work with it. Disgust, anger and contempt are the usual feelings to emerge, together with a sense of outrage at the waste involved, both in terms of the amount of money spent on food and also the expense of time and energy on what can appear to be such a pointless symptom. The health care professionals on the courses we have taught have expressed all these feelings, together sometimes with a sense of envy at the pseudo-solution which bulimia appears to be. Bulimic women, eating huge amounts of food and yet staying slim, appear to be getting away with it!

For many people, bulimia seems like a metaphor for the age we live in; successful, privileged women want to be able to eat, to gorge themselves on food, without paying the price in terms of becoming fat. The wastefulness which is such an enraging feature of bulimia for many people can also be interpreted as a consequence of the affluence and narcissism of our age, an age which values youth, appearance and affluence above all else. Bulimia is a very common symptom for women. It could also be considered to be a particularly accurate reflection of the way many women in our culture at this time relate to themselves and the world, by placing all their trust in their appearance at the expense of their feelings and their health. However, from a psychological point of view, its meanings seem to be more complex and far-reaching than would appear on the surface.

In Chapter 1 we suggested that in order to understand eating disorders we need to take into account not only the pattern of disordered eating itself, but also its effects on the woman's body. Bulimia – eating followed by self-induced vomiting – is unlike other eating disorders in that its effects are generally invisible. In the case of anorexia and compulsive eating, women are using their bodies to express the way they feel about themselves and their relation to the social world. The compulsive eater, through her fat, shows that she hates and despises herself. The fat indicates her feeling that she cannot and will not conform to the social expectation that as a woman she must be in perfect control and hide the needy part of herself. The anorexic, by her thinness, makes a statement that in order to be the perfect, controlled, needless creature she believes people want, she must put herself in mortal danger. Bulimic women are generally, though not always, quite unexceptional in terms of their size and weight. It is usually quite striking, at the start of a group or workshop for bulimic women, to look around the room and see a collection of such apparently 'normal' women, who look for all the world as though they don't have a problem between them.

Although many bulimic women live in fear of becoming

overweight, they are not generally fearful of normal weight, as anorexics are. Most say they would rather deal with their fears by abstaining from food as the anorexic woman does, but generally they do not. It is only when the bulimic woman comes to decode and understand the meanings of her own behaviour that she can see why she has 'chosen' this particular way of expressing her distress and what it says about her internal world. The crucial point about the symptom of bulimia is that it expresses the desperate attempts of the woman to appear to be 'normal', to completely hide and disguise the distressed part of herself so that only she has access to it, via her symptom.

In the case of bulimia, the woman's problems do not show on her body. Her body actually belies the fact that she has a problem around food. The bulimic woman expresses her distress not through her body, but through her disordered pattern of eating. The key which unlocks the hidden meaning of bulimia lies in the striking juxtaposition of the woman's well-organized life as it appears on the surface and her bizarre and secretive behaviour around food. This is reflected by the discrepancy between her 'normal'-looking body and her feelings about herself as anything but 'normal'.

Most of the bulimic women we have worked with are very good 'copers'. More than most women, they set a high store by managing their lives competently and cheerfully. Some of them are particularly successful in their careers, often also running a home and caring for a family. They are women who rarely make demands on family and friends and often take more than their fair share of other people's troubles. They really are the kind of women who are admired for their capacity to keep everything running smoothly. Yet underneath this trouble-free exterior, the woman expresses secretly the part of herself which is not coping at all.

Harriet was twenty-eight when she first acknowledged that she had a problem and came to ask for help. She was married with two small daughters and worked part-time as a yoga teacher. Her husband had a successful business and Harriet supported him, keeping the books and entertaining his friends. Financially they were quite secure, and Harriet described her relationship with her husband as 'close and supportive'. Every morning she would get the girls ready for school, lunches packed, husband's breakfast on the table. She would drive her daughters to school and on her way home would stop at the shops to buy food. But it was not food for the family that she bought. She was a good cook and very health-conscious, but each morning she bought chocolate, cream, ice cream, Coca-Cola and biscuits. Returning to her kitchen, she ate and ate until it was all gone. Then she would go up to the bathroom and throw it all up again. On days when she did not have a class in the afternoon, she might buy more food and repeat the process all over again. Everything would be cleaned up, the house tidy and welcoming by the time the children came home. If her husband was working late, then after supervising the children's homework and getting them off to bed, she might again binge and make herself sick until she finally went to sleep, exhausted. No one at all knew how she spent her days.

Now if Harriet had consciously been very unhappy, it might have seemed easier to understand her behaviour. But she herself was not aware of anything in her life which was really wrong. The only problem she could identify was her compulsion to over-eat and make herself sick. She felt deeply ashamed of herself and sure that this guilty secret was spoiling her whole life. She felt that her husband and friends would be shocked and horrified if they knew her secret. In her professional life, she knew she gave the impression not only of being competent but also of being very stable and 'sorted out'. She encouraged her students to practise yoga to relax and produce a sense of well-being, yet she herself had to resort to this bizarre and self-destructive pattern to get her through the day. It was unthinkable to Harriet that anyone should ever find out. If they were to do so, she would be revealed as a fraud and a charlatan. The idea that she could not manage her own life properly, that she might need help, seemed appalling to her. This split between the conscious, coping part of the self and the hidden, non-coping part which is largely unconscious is very typical of bulimia. The symptom serves to keep this non-coping part unknown to the woman herself. She simply does not know the part of her which is in such distress and which causes her so much trouble. She thinks the bulimia is her only problem.

By looking carefully at the symptom which the woman produces, we can begin to learn something about this unknown part of her. The guilt she experiences shows us clearly that this is a part of herself of which she feels deeply ashamed. It is a very violent and destructive piece of behaviour, a means of discharging all these unwanted impulses. In the process of vomiting, the woman repeatedly makes a mess, which she carefully cleans up time and time again. The messy, out of control part of herself is thus contained and enacted by the symptom and can be denied in the more conscious and visible aspects of her life. She tries to use her bulimia as a kind of dustbin into which she can put everything which is not perfect, agreeable and controlled.

The symptom also tells us something else. It is no coincidence that she expresses this split off and denied part of herself via food and eating. Instead of feeling distress, she feels an uncontrollable appetite. These feelings throw her into chaos and she tries to satisfy herself by cramming food into her mouth. As soon as she has eaten and come into touch with her needy, violent, devouring self, she is filled with guilt and feels an urgent desire to rid herself of what she has eaten. The end result of the bulimia, the eating and vomiting, is that the woman feels empty and entirely without needs. This is precisely the feeling she is seeking; she feels empty, relaxed and achieves a kind of peace. Of course, she feels guilty and ashamed, but this is a feeling she is quite used to and now all of these feelings are focused firmly on her symptom. In a limited way, bulimia achieves for her what she wants. The split off, unwanted part of herself is contained in the symptom, leaving the rest of her life free from trouble and distress. The problem with this solution is that she has a continual sense of cheating, of achieving everything in a fraudulent way. Everything she actually does is undermined for her by the means she uses to achieve it.

In Harriet's case, this problem had a long history. Soon after she was born, her father developed a serious mental illness from which he never really recovered. Harriet's mother tried her hardest to protect her and her younger brother from her father's odd and sometimes alarming behaviour. Basically, she carried on as if nothing was really wrong. Harriet spent long periods of time with her aunt, never being quite sure when she would be going home. Not only did she have to deal with her own sense of rejection and anxiety, but she also had to answer questions from children and teachers at school about the rather unusual arrangements in her family. She could never tell anyone what was really going on. Indeed, she did not know; she was never allowed and never allowed herself to know what her father's and her family's problems were. As a child, she had terrifying fantasies about the nature of her father's illness and the safety of her mother and brother. In spite of all this, she was expected by her mother and her aunt to 'cope' and to carry on as though everything was all right. She learnt to split off and hide the distressed part of herself, to disown and deny it. This theme of a woman being led to construct her own life around a guilty secret in the family is a common feature in the histories of bulimic women.

When she was fifteen, things began to become too much for Harriet. She became increasingly withdrawn and preoccupied with herself, her body and her weight. She lost weight, but managed to avoid it becoming dangerously low. Her family did not take her problems too seriously. They regarded it as a 'phase' which she would grow out of. She did appear to recover and managed to carry on, passing her exams and gaining a place at university. It was while she was studying that she first began to use the symptom of bulimia. For her it contained not only the distressed, lonely and needy part of her which had to be covered up, but also the part of her which she experienced as crazy, irrational, out of control – the part, in fact, which represented her father.

When Harriet met her husband, she hoped that the loving, supportive relationship which he offered would solve her problems for her and would help her to break her self-destructive pattern. Again, the births of her children were intended, but failed to put things right. She took up yoga in an attempt to find a more positive means of dealing with her disturbed feelings. She became very good at yoga and eventually trained as a teacher, but still her bulimia intermittently continued. It was as though the adult part of her personality had continued in some sense to grow and develop so that she was able to acquire skills and make relationships, at least superficially. Beneath this, however, the frightened, needy, chaotic part of her, representing her childhood, still remained, unable to show itself and unable to get any help. Whatever Harriet did, either personally or professionally, she never seemed to get anything out of it for herself. She could look after her family, teach yoga to other people, but she never had a sense of being taken care of or of being able to take proper care of herself.

In the personal histories of women who suffer from bulimia,

we often find that there have been real objective difficulties within the family. Often, as children, bulimic women have suffered separation from parents by divorce or death. These difficult events, though in themselves inherently problematic for a developing child to negotiate, have usually been made very much worse by pressures on the child to deny and repress all the feelings they have engendered. Time and again, we see the pattern of cutting off from troubled feelings, acting as though everything is really all right when clearly it is not.

These are families who often consider it 'bad' to have and express powerful and painful feelings, families who set a high premium on coping, covering up, carrying on. As we will see later on, women in our society are usually brought up to minimize their own disturbed and chaotic feelings. Very early on in life, before they are really able to handle and contain their own anxiety, mothers tend to expect their daughters not to make a fuss. The bulimic woman is therefore struggling to be good. She will go to any lengths to present only the 'good' side of herself and to split off and conceal the 'bad'.

Jekyll and Hyde

The well-known fictional story of Dr Jekyll and Mr Hyde illustrates the attempts of one man to keep his good and bad elements separate and apart. Dr Jekyll was a famous doctor, renowned for his good works and his friendly and generous nature. However, he felt that his goodness could not be pure and perfect if he had any human flaws, any 'bad' thoughts, feelings or actions. In order to be sure of his own goodness, he felt compelled to invent a potion which would separate the good person within him from the bad. By the use of this drug, the bad part of him was encapsulated in a nightly counterpart to the daytime man. This 'night' person ventured out secretly, through the back door, to involve himself in minor misdemeanours as a different man – Mr Hyde.

In this way, he hoped that his good side could be perfectly good and that his bad side, totally separated, would be incapable of spoiling that perfection. Life, however, is not that simple. The closer Dr Jekyll came to perfection, the more cruel, vicious and out of control his nightly opponent became. Then, one day, the monster inside no longer waited to be invited out by the drug. He became an independent man, who came unbidden, present for longer and longer periods, more in charge of things, more monstrous and more cruel. The parallels with bulimia are obvious. The important point here is to remember that the bulimic woman's original impetus for creating her monstrous symptom is as an attempt to be good.

Like Dr Jekyll, the part of herself which she condemns as bad contains nothing more sinister than her feelings – her anger, her sexual feelings, her hatred, envy, dependence and neediness. At times strong feelings including happiness and intense feelings of love can also seem dangerous and disturbing. Such feelings can have the effect of making the woman feel irrational and out of control. These feelings too have to be split off and denied.

While hiding the distressed, 'bad' part of herself, the bulimic woman longs to show it. That is why she so often repeats her terrifying ritual around food. Over and over again she confronts herself with the part of her she so hates and despises. She cannot show it to other people, but it is as though she is saying silently to her family, her friends, 'This is what I am really like. This is what you have done to me. This is what you make me do.' Her symptom also contains a powerful message about what she thinks of anyone's attempts to nurture her; it is rubbish, it is bad, she throws it up. The food, which symbolizes both her attempts at self-nurture and the attempts of others to take effective care of her, turns bad inside her. It makes her feel weak, dependent and even more needy than before. By rejecting the food and feeling triumphant in its rejection, she achieves a kind of self-sufficiency which makes her feel as though she doesn't need anyone. She feels so bad inside that when the food comes into contact with this badness, it becomes bad and turns to poison inside her.

Mess and creativity

In common with most women in our society, bulimic women are preoccupied with coping, covering up and keeping their lives tidy and organized. Being tidy, keeping things tidy and clearing up mess are very central aspects of the traditional role of women. Women themselves are expected to be neat, tidy and controlled, not only in their appearance but in their behaviour and demeanour as well. One of the most insulting things that can be said about a woman is that she is 'a mess'! One of the consequences of this is that women generally are very frightened when their inner worlds feel messy, confused and out of control. Unruly feelings, which are often judged inappropriate, can make women feel as though there is a terrible, frightening mess inside them which has to be cleared up, sorted out and hidden away. Bulimia is a means of dealing with this internal mess. Instead of being able to have her own confused, messy, childlike feelings, she tries to soothe them away with food and then violently rejects them, throws them out as rubbish. By vomiting and literally making a mess, the woman maintains a sense of being able to control her messy internal world. She can expel it and get rid of it at will. The symptom of bulimia enables the woman to believe that all her messy and out of control feelings can be contained within it.

The psychoanalyst D. W. Winnicott writes of the importance of what he calls 'potential space'. Potential space is the area of overlap where the personal inner world of the individual comes into contact with the external world of shared reality. This, according to Winnicott, is the area in which children play. This is the area in which the inner world of the child finds expression in the shared world of culture. This potential space is also the area in which adult creativity occurs. In order to be creative, it is necessary to have a free space in which internal reality can tentatively encounter the external world and begin to make something new which both reflects the inner reality and expresses it in the terms of the cultural world. Sometimes children become so anxious and distressed that they simply cannot play. There seems to be no space in which it is safe to allow their inner worlds to emerge and come creatively into contact with the world. Adults too can lose or fail to develop potential creative space. The external world impinges so much that the inner world has to be tightly locked up and kept in. It is within this potential space that the symptom of bulimia occurs. This is not to say that bulimia is really a form of creativity, but that the bulimia occupies the same space in the woman's life as her potential creativity. Her internal world is so frightening and chaotic that in the space where she should be able to express her creativity she instead develops a self-destructive symptom. Instead of being able to express some of the chaos and mess she feels inside herself, she ruthlessly tries to get rid of it.

Order and disorder

The disordered pattern of the bulimic woman's eating expresses the sense of internal disorder she feels. Eating is generally a social activity, quite strictly regulated by rules and conventions. The bulimic woman defies and makes a mockery of all these conventions. She eats raw food which should be cooked, frozen food, dry pasta. Her eating is utterly chaotic. She eats standing up, with her hands. There is no order, there are no rules, no conventions. The bulimic woman's eating is a kind of ritual of disorder, which she repeats over and over again. Often the process of cleaning up after the bulimic episode also has a ritual quality about it and if she is interrupted while she is vomiting or cleaning up she is filled with anxiety and despair. The disorder which is being acted out in this way shows clearly how she experiences her own inner world. Deep within herself there remains hidden a part of her which is full of a terrifying chaos and confusion. In this part of her there are no boundaries, no categories. One thing spills over into another, she feels as though nothing can be contained. It is a part of her which she experiences as savage, primitive and uncivilized. In a more profound sense, she feels as though something is deeply wrong with her, something which makes her defy all social niceties. In a curious way, the bulimic woman delights in her ritual of disorder. She expresses through it her fury with the world and her refusal to give up the part of herself which is in touch with the confused, hurt and furious child in her.

Relationships

The bulimic woman is terrified of intimacy. All her relationships are characterized by this terror. She shows the same ambivalence towards people as she shows to food. While she craves to be close to someone and to be loved, she lives in fear of being 'found out', of her façade being shattered, revealing the real 'bad' person underneath. When she does find herself in the close relationship she has been looking for, she will often develop an immediate aversion to the person. She may feel trapped and impelled to seek her 'independence'. Her needs drive her into a relationship but then she is driven out of it by her fears.

Fighting Food

Often the bulimic woman will show her fear of intimacy by having several relationships at once. None of them really satisfies, yet she cannot find a way of giving any of them up. She cannot bear to put all her eggs in one basket. She dreads being smothered, taken over by a relationship. This terror of being devoured, of losing the self in a relationship, alternates with a wish completely to consume the other person. The bulimic woman often feels her love and neediness to be dangerous. She is afraid not only of being devoured but also of her own wish to devour. Food becomes a safe way of dealing with these conflicting impulses. On the one hand she devours huge quantities of food and thereby gains control of it and destroys it. By vomiting it up she is refusing to let it damage her or take her over. She pushes it out before it can do so.

Her moods and attitudes to the world and to other people may change dramatically. At times she may be compulsively active and sociable, at other times depressed, withdrawn and solitary. Both of these ways of being effectively prevent her from making deep and satisfying relationships. They are different ways of ensuring that she is never really close to anyone or known by anyone. Most women who suffer from bulimia frequently retreat into a fantasy of a time, somewhere in the future, when everything will be different. In this fantasy, the woman will find someone who truly loves her, she will be able to be loved and her bulimia will disappear. Her life will fall into place, she will no longer have to hide herself within the secret prison which she has created for herself.

In fact, of course, it is by acknowledging the feelings which the bulimia gets rid of that she will be able to feel more real and able to be loved. The fantasy she holds on to reinforces her view that it is the bulimia which stops her from achieving what she wants. If only she can rid herself of this horrible obsession she will be able to blossom into the kind of person she really wants to be. In reality, it is exactly the other way round. It is because she feels deep down that she is horrible and bad that she is in such an impossible situation. The bulimia is merely her way of expressing this self-hatred.

NOTES

For a detailed account of the issues involved in bulimia, together with suggestions for change, see M. Dana and M. Lawrence (1988): *Women's Secret Disorder*, Grafton, London.

5
WOMEN IN THE WORLD

There can be no doubt that eating disorders are problems which predominantly affect women. There are very few psychological problems which show such a marked preference for one sex, and in order to understand the current epidemic of eating disorders, it is vital to begin by considering just why this should be so. Throughout this chapter we will be looking at the different worlds which women inhabit and analysing the contradictions inherent in them. It is our contention that women's day-to-day reality is fraught with conflicts – some obvious, others less obvious – which predispose women towards difficulties with food.

Women's social situation – the legacy of the past

A woman in our society is still in many respects a second-class citizen. She is considered an inferior person in terms of her intellectual capacity, her occupation, her contribution to society and her role in the family. Even though things are changing and have greatly shifted in the last twenty years, 'feminine' occupations still tend to be valued less highly than masculine ones.

Women are still secretaries while a man is usually the 'boss' in business and industry; while many women now enter medicine, far fewer men are interested in becoming nurses. Some of the jobs carrying both the lowest status and the lowest wages, such as cleaning, and caring for children and the elderly, are done almost exclusively by women. In spite of the enormous increase in opportunities for women, we still find very few women in positions of power and influence. Only 6 per cent of Members of Parliament are women, 3 per cent of ambassadors, 7 per cent of senior civil servants and 3 per cent of university professors. It seems as though, in spite of women now being represented in almost every walk of life, it is still correct to think of the policy-makers and the very high fliers in most professions as men.

In our own culture there is still a very strong tendency to believe that womanhood equals motherhood. Most girls are brought up to think of themselves as mothers of the future and to believe that in some sense this is the proper or 'natural' role for women to take on. This early socialization into the mother's role means that it is hard for women to have a sense of themselves as independent people in the world. Even the woman who doesn't have children, who perhaps has a prestigious job of her own, may still feel that she is missing out on her 'proper' role. We often find that women who are quite successful in their own right nonetheless behave like mothers towards their friends or colleagues, always feeling that they must consider the needs of others before their own. Motherhood is a powerful concept which affects all women.

Motherhood is often seen not as a form of work but as an alternative to work. For those women who occupy more traditional roles, the hard work they do at home – cleaning, cooking, mothering and answering needs – is often not considered work at all, especially not as labour worthy of wages. 'What does your mother do?' we are asked at school time and time again. The answer is always: 'Nothing, she is just a housewife.' Being a housewife is not being anything. Being a mother to three or four children is not enough as a full-time occupation. Women do not get formally paid for this hard work. Within a traditional family structure, women are expected to be financially dependent on a man.

This financial dependence causes day-to-day emotional and intellectual dependence. All the woman's wishes, or at least the major ones, are censored in order to gain her husband's acceptance of them. If she wishes to go on a course, take a holiday, go to university, buy clothes or anything for herself, she has to have the approval of the person who earns the money – usually the man.

A woman who has no man to support her is dependent on the state. As she has no means of having her children taken care of, she has no option but to exist on a very low level of state 'welfare' benefits, with very little choice as to how to lead her life.

What does it mean to be a mother and a housewife? It means primarily to be attentive to other people's needs. Much of this nurturing is expressed through the provision of food. She has to know what her family likes to eat and cook it for them, to know what is bothering them and how to attend to it. When her husband comes home from work tired, food should be ready and the house clean – no one expects that she too will be tired. The mother's needs are not as important as those of others. It is assumed that because she has not worked hard outside the home all day she should serve those who have. So after a day of serving in the family's absence she has to serve them in their presence.

We do recognize that many things have changed. Working outside the home may lessen a woman's actual material dependence. Some women are now free to choose to bring up children on their own or within a lesbian couple. Women recognize their rights much more. But in many places the reality is still traditional and it is obvious that our mothers' generation has not provided us with a very useful alternative model, so these stereotypes are still here with us, affecting our vision and experience of ourselves and of other women.

Women and food

One of the most powerful features characterizing the traditional role of the woman is the intimate association she has with food. In most households, whatever their form or composition, it is a woman who takes prime and often sole responsibility for the provision of food. This does not just mean cooking; many men cook. But how many men feel responsible when the cornflakes run out? The planning of meals, budgeting, shopping, preparing and generally monitoring the state of the store cupboard take up many hours each week of most women's time. It is generally women, not men, who are to be found shopping in the lunch hour; women's magazines, not men's, which contain all the recipes; and women who organize the day's activities around providing a family meal.

But what do women buy and cook and how do they decide? With an ever-increasing range and variety of foods from which to choose, a vast industry has grown up to try to promote one sort of food over another. Women are the almost exclusive targets of all this propaganda, and much of it exploits the already conflicting feelings which women have about the task. Women have the responsibility not only for keeping the family happy, but also for their health. Should children have the sweets and sugary cereals they ask for? Mother will probably get no thanks for providing a low-fat, low-sugar, high-fibre diet. Although women have more control over the provision of food than perhaps anything else in their lives, it is very hard indeed for them to get it right.

The other side of women's role as providers of food is the powerful social injunction that women themselves should not eat very much at all. While the beautifully and expensively packaged processed foods are aimed at tempting the appetites of 'the family', it is the ever-increasing range of slimming foods which are targeted at women themselves. The contradiction is encapsulated nowhere more clearly than in the weekly women's magazines. We are confronted with pages of mouth-watering pictures ('tempting recipes for the family') only to find them followed by a six-page supplement for the woman herself ('getting in shape for summer/spring/Christmas'). Finally, we are presented with pictures of clothes hanging on models who look so skinny that one can hardly believe they eat at all.

This contradictory relationship which women have with food really symbolizes their role within the family. Women's own needs, desires and appetites are considered unimportant and secondary in relation to those of others. While attending to the needs of others, she must keep herself and her own wishes and needy feelings under control. Her priority, while looking after others, is to keep herself slim, attractive and acceptable. This emphasis on appearance as the central feature of a woman's identity is another vital factor which can predispose women towards eating disorders.

Self-image

By self-image we mean the way each individual perceives and thinks about herself or himself. Self-image is complex; it is built up of a number of different factors, such as intelligence, competence and attractiveness. For the majority of women, however, appearance is probably the most important element in self-image.

For many women, and especially those who go on to develop an eating disorder, self-image (the way we perceive ourselves) centres around body-image (the internal picture we have of our own bodies). In *Fat is a Feminist Issue*, Susie Orbach quotes Schilder's definition of body image as 'the picture of our own body which we form in our minds, that is to say the way in which the body appears to ourselves'.[1] This is an integrated concept built up from all sensory and psychic experiences. In women, self-image and body-image are usually quite consistent. The woman who dislikes her own body and feels bad about it usually has a poor self-image and feels bad about herself. Certain body shapes and sizes are imbued by society with particular characteristics. Children are very sensitive and receptive to the attitudes of others. The child who is plump may well come to think of herself as lazy and stupid if other people treat her in this way. In racist societies, children from despised ethnic groups often grow up believing not only that they are inferior to the dominant group, but also that their bodies are unattractive because they are different. It is difficult to really love and be proud of one's own body if one is constantly presented with images of bodies quite different from one's own which are deemed to be attractive and desirable. Body image is thus over-emphasized and, even worse, the media become a source of control over values – what is beautiful, who is perfect and who is successful. Those who do not match the socially acceptable image find themselves under enormous pressure and constant criticism.

Western contemporary society is obsessed with slimness to the point of overtly condemning women who are obese, fat or overweight to any extent. This is seen nowhere more clearly than when any female member of the British royal family, who can usually do no wrong in the eyes of the popular press, is thought to have gained weight. The press suddenly becomes ruthless in its condemnation of the woman, employing every means at its disposal to ridicule and humiliate her, with exhortations to her to change her ways. This quite clearly is what the public wants to read and represents widely held attitudes towards fat women. They are considered ugly, unattractive, undesirable, and failures as women.

The condemnation of fat people goes beyond their appearance. Research on the attitudes of very young children shows that from an early age, children learn to prefer images of thin children. In fact, children from despised racial groups and children with disabilities or disfigurements are preferred to fat children. When asked what is wrong with fat children, the most common answers given by their peers are that they are lazy, stupid and lonely. These are the associations which remain with us throughout our lives.

Characteristics associated with slenderness include beauty, grace and femininity as well as shrewdness, gentleness, dignity and success. Some negative ideas, such as coldness and selfishness, are sometimes attached to slimness, but beauty always is. Therefore many fat women, especially those who have carried their overweight for years (since adolescence or childhood), speak with real anguish of their terrible shape – of their disgustingly fat, ugly, loathsome bodies.

It is important to stress that body-image is by no means an accurate picture. Many women see themselves as fat and unattractive, while other people may be quite unaware of their real or imagined 'imperfections'. It is probably true to say that all women with eating disorders have a distorted body-image, in that they experience their bodies quite differently from the way they are perceived by others. The tendency is usually to feel themselves to be fatter than they really are, and with this sense of being fat go all the negative characteristics which undermine the woman's sense of self.

Body-image is not necessarily constant. A characteristic common to all overweight women, and to many other women who are not objectively overweight, is that they experience their bodies as fluctuating and distorted according to their moods on different days, and in different situations. Looking in a mirror – which is supposed to be an objective experience, conveying always the same physical size – is experienced by overweight women as reflecting a variety of images on different occasions. Moreover, especially with very obese women, their appearance is distorted. They will either see themselves as bigger than they are, enormous, without limits, or they will see themselves as a lot smaller than they appear to others and how they are in reality. At times of stress, a woman who does not normally feel herself to be fat may find herself becoming dissatisfied with her body. She then blames the way she feels on her 'fat' body. At other times, when she is feeling more confident, she will see herself more realistically.

Women in a compulsive eating group (some very large, others not especially overweight) were asked to draw themselves as they saw their own bodies without clothes. The mere fact that several women had obviously not seen themselves in the mirror naked and could not draw themselves with no clothes on reflects some of the difficulties they experience in relation to their body-image. Some drew themselves with clothes on; some side-ways so as to show themselves in a thinner position; some drew hands that covered their bellies; some did not have enough space on the whole page for certain limbs or parts of their bodies; some drew themselves very small in the centre or at the corner of the page.

Some women who are very overweight unconsciously protect their self-image by disowning the fat, as if they are saying: 'This is not me – I am the thin person within who has little to do with this enormous figure looking at me from that mirror.' Thus while they are aware of being fat, they simultaneously hold on to the idea that the 'real' person inside is thin.

Our deeply held attitudes towards fat and thin women are illustrated by an exercise done by a group of professional women and men who were asked to create a life story around a picture of a fat woman, followed by a thin woman. Most of the stories created for the fat woman portrayed her as lonely, unpopular, badly dressed, never having fun or going on holiday. The life stories created around the thin woman, on the other hand, were all of someone very successful and happy, with a family and a rich social life.

The unconscious advantages of being fat

We have been looking at the ways in which a woman's feelings about her body colour and to a large extent determine how she feels about herself. We must also consider that a woman with a very poor self-image may use her body as a means of expressing her feelings about herself.

Fat is a Feminist Issue was the first book written for women themselves which suggested that women might unconsciously make themselves fat. This can be a difficult idea for women to accept. Consciously, they hate being fat and will go to any lengths to lose weight. However, as we saw in Esther's story in Chapter 3, there can be powerful unconscious motives for being or staying fat. The advantages of being fat are that it adds substance, gives boundaries, and pushes people away. It both expresses and hides a sense of emptiness and inner fragility. Feeling fragile leads women to put on weight to protect themselves. Feeling empty in spirit, emotion and intellect brings women to put on weight to feel more substantial. In order to protect herself from others' anger, hostility, hatred and demands – to push others away from her – the fat woman builds a wall around her, a boundary based on fear of being engulfed. It is as though a firmness of body and strength of muscle will counter the fear of losing herself. There is also a certain way of wearing clothes that is associated with the overweight woman – being uncaring, wearing scruffy clothes as if to say 'I'm so fat, what's the point?' and wearing very large shapeless dresses to hide her figure; and particular ways that she will sit and present her body in social situations – with arms and legs folded, enclosed within herself.

Anorexia and self-image

Anorexia can be understood as a desperate attempt to improve or to cover up a very poor self-image. The woman who develops anorexia has no real belief in herself. She is anxious and unsure about her own capabilities and often carries within her a profound sense of being bad. She attempts to use her body to solve these problems and to prove to herself and others that she is a strong, independent and worthwhile person. The anorexic does not simply want to be thin to make herself attractive. What she really covets are the personality characteristics which are associated with being thin. Here we can see again the way in which, in contemporary Western society, women's bodies have become the focus of so much conflict and discontent. In order to be 'good', the woman feels she must perfect her body. It is as though nothing else matters. Most anorexics report that in the early stages of their difficulties, when they first began to lose weight, they were rewarded by admiration from friends and family. To be able to lose weight, to control one's body and force it to change, is regarded as a sign of health and strength and is greatly admired.

Bulimia and self-image

For the bulimic woman the issue of her self-image and body-image is again quite a complicated one. Looking, as she does, quite 'normal' or ordinary, her body does not indicate her problems. When looking at a bulimic woman, unlike an anorexic or compulsive eater, one would not know or suspect that she has a problem with food. Yet underneath the ordinary façade is hidden a very poor self-image that has no anchor in reality. She has no reason to be dissatisfied with her body and yet inside she feels awful about herself, disgusting and out of control. She has a guilty horrible secret: her bulimia, which she feels is the reason for all her problems, makes her unattractive and hateful and must be kept secret. If anyone were to find out, they would feel about that part of herself the way she does – rejecting, repulsed, violent. She has no hope or expectation that anyone may feel compassion or acceptance towards this part of her. They will leave her, condemn and blame her, which is what she feels she deserves.

The bulimic woman thus presents an acceptable image to the world, but it is an image which she does not believe in. Her self-image could hardly be more different from the favourable impression she makes on others.

Femininity

Femininity is a difficult notion to discuss. In one sense, femininity and masculinity are always social constructions. They amount to no more or less than the attributes which any society ascribes to women and men. It is impossible to know or even to think about what would be considered masculine or feminine outside of a social context. On the other hand, there does seem to be a constancy through time of what is regarded as feminine. What changes, however, is the way in which feminine characteristics are valued.

Femininity, the female energy – the 'anima' – has been worshipped at times and devalued at others. The values put upon women and the attitudes towards them have also altered through time, but the traits associated with femininity remain the same. These traits or characteristics can potentially be interpreted and responded to in positive or negative ways. The same feminine energy, way of life and feelings that are powerful in matriarchal societies lose much of their potency and power in a patriarchal society. A woman is expected to be passive, receptive, waiting, emotional, submissive, subservient and seductive. Not only have such traits become expected of individual women rather than simply part of an archetypal feminine, but negative values have also been placed on them. 'Emotional' becomes equated with 'hysterical', 'receptive' becomes 'reactive' (non-active), 'passive' becomes 'weak, powerless', waiting becomes not initiating, and submissive comes to mean accepting anything that comes along.

In our society, femininity is often interpreted in these ways and so-called feminine qualities are generally regarded with contempt.

In reality, however, one can be receptive yet choose what to take in and what to refuse. One can be receptive and active, not just a reactor, and emotional or vulnerable does not have to mean hysterical or out of control.

As well as devaluing feminine characteristics, our culture generally fosters derogatory attitudes towards women's bodies, which women themselves internalize and reproduce. Menstruation is one of the most tangible expressions of femininity, and looking at how it is regarded can give us some insight into attitudes towards feminine powers. It has particular relevance in the case of anorexia, in which one of the symptoms is that menstruation ceases.

In some cultures of the past, women's awareness of their bodies was directed inward. They were not expected to be externally beautiful: their well-being, acceptability and success were not determined by nor expressed through how they looked. A woman was aware of her body and the relationship of its cycles to those of nature. She was the Amazon. Menstruation was part of her natural cycle and not something to be ashamed of. Rituals and ceremonies in which women got together to experience and encourage this inner consciousness were common.

In *The Wise Wound*, Penelope Shuttle and Peter Redgrove say:

> There is no reason why Everywoman should not consciously inhabit the kingdom of her body from which she has been exiled by male certitudes which are called 'objective' but which are often the turning-away from unexpected powers and abilities ... The phases of the cycle *can* work in harmony. The effects of its rhythms can be to stimulate and to show up facets of one's nature. Menstruation is usually treated as a dustbin in which all the unwanted bits are put by the women as well as the men ...[2]

But in more recent times, in religious as well as social conventions, women have been excluded from the activities of ordinary life while menstruating. For centuries women were told that their menstruating bodies were unacceptable not only to men but also to God. The association of menstruation with guilt and shame remains powerful today. Religious and non-religious women alike experience the oppressive feeling that when they are menstruating they are doing something wrong. (Only 100 years ago girls in England were told that they should stay out of the dairy while they were menstruating lest they turn the milk sour.)

For girls this means believing right from the start that what happens in their bodies is disgusting and must be kept secret. Menstruation is common to all women, but girls are made to experience it as their own private problem, a shameful personal affliction which they must deal with alone. It is not hard to see how the name 'the curse' has survived. Girls have been taught to endure anxiety and physical discomfort as their lot. One woman expressed this attitude when talking about her first experience with menstruation: 'My mother took me to the bathroom, locked the door, and with a very secretive voice she told me, "Be careful not to use the same soap as your father and brother while you are on, as they might become sterile."'

This attitude is crucial when talking about femininity. With such a grim picture placed before her, it would be surprising if a girl was able to love and be proud of emerging femininity. In her book *The Owl Was a Baker's Daughter*, Marion Woodman writes:

> One thing seems clear. Where the mother was unquestionably in touch with her femininity, she has given to her daughter a love of being a woman and a basic faith in life. Where the mother is negative, the daughter is from the beginning hampered in making emotional adjustments and fails to take the natural steps toward feminine maturity ... The child who is not allowed to live her own spontaneous rhythms develops a petrifying fear of the power of her own instincts because she is cut off from her own inner being, and therefore cut off from the reality of life. Such a child becomes an adult woman who simply does not comprehend the feminine principle. For her 'being negative' means surrendering control ... and the consequences could be fatal ... Better to try to keep control by remaining silent and acting out the roles of daughter, wife, and mother as she has always half-heartedly understood them. Indeed she may be making the only choice she can ... She suffers the humiliation of her self-deception and probably turns to identification with the evil food ... The thing in her which should live is alone. Nobody touches it, nobody knows it, she herself doesn't know it. But it keeps on stirring, it disturbs her, it makes her restless, it gives her no peace.[3]

This issue of femininity and respect for her own body, instincts, emotions and womanhood is very important for both compulsive eaters and anorexics. One of the physical symptoms of anorexia is the loss of periods, so as well as looking like a young girl or boy rather than a woman, the anorexic annihilates the manifestation of her unwanted femininity – menstruation. She rejects it and feels powerful through this rejection, even if consciously she feels worried by the loss of her periods. She has fought yet another inner weakness and won. She is special – she can even control her own biological functions, which most women must accept whether they want to or not. She is ultimately clean, having triumphed over dirty physical processes.

For the compulsive eater, femininity is also nothing to be proud of, though the issue is not as harsh and clear-cut as with the anorexic. Her body to her does not usually seem feminine. Frequently her low self-image is centred in her body. She feels no one ever really loves her for who she is, and her body is one expression (as well as a cause) of that feeling. She therefore finds it frightening to lose herself in a relationship, so instead she does it with food. Her ideas about femininity usually centre on mothering other people (overweight women are often seen as 'motherly'), and she finds it difficult to separate motherliness from femininity and vice versa. Femininity is therefore identified with 'mother-like', but this equation does not allow her to work out what it means to be feminine apart from being motherly.

Another conflictual aspect of femininity which finds a form of expression in eating disorders is the social equation of 'feminine' with neat, clean, tidy and well-organized. In our culture, it is simply not feminine to be messy. From an early age, little girls not only observe their mothers cleaning up after other people and keeping everything in order, but they themselves are encouraged to be tidy and clean. In truth, of course, all human nature and activity has its messy side, but the idea that to be feminine means to eradicate this gives women particular problems. At the level of the body, they feel they must always appear neat; the messy aspects of the female body are despised and every attempt is made to ensure that they are concealed. Menstruation in particular is despised and feared as a manifestation of the messy aspects of femininity. In a psychological sense, women are encouraged to feel that they must be able to 'hold everything together', which very often means keeping everything within themselves; in particular, disorderly feelings which would upset or embarrass other people have to be kept in, or sometimes denied to the extent that they are not even felt.

Eating disorders can be powerful mechanisms for dealing with this unwanted part of the self. In anorexia, everything needy and emotional is split off and denied. The anorexic gives the appearance of being perfectly calm, contained and in control of herself. Even her body has lost its feminine messiness. In bulimia, the whole unruly, unacceptable part of the woman's personality is contained within the symptom. It is hidden away and enacted in secret. The bulimic woman often thinks of herself as having an awful, disgusting, shameful part, which has to be concealed. From our point of view, it is actually an aspect of her femininity which she finds so frightening and which needs to be controlled and hidden.

The question of control

Control is a central preoccupation for women with eating disorders. One of the most frequently voiced fears is of being out of control. Although the struggle for control centres on the body and very specifically on food intake, there are great underlying anxieties about control which permeate all aspects of women's lives.

Any sort of conflict can lead a woman to feel she is out of control, drifting between two identities, two decisions, two modes of being. This feeling can bring her to look desperately for any area in which she can feel totally, or at least partly, in control. Paradoxically, while feeling that she is not in control of her body, the woman may well feel that she does have a great deal of control over the provision of food. This is connected to a woman's function, in our society, of nurturing, feeding and being the 'mistress of the family' concerning food. She is the one who knows how much groceries cost and where to buy what. She is the one who is supposed to buy all food and kitchen accessories. She is the one who dictates what and when the family will eat – in short, she is the one who controls all food issues.

She transposes the lack of control in other areas into this area and, instead of attempting to gain more power in other areas of her life, she increases her control here. This is one area, then, in which she can sometimes be free to do as she likes and to have control over those closest to her. It is understandable, therefore, that this is the first and most immediate area in which she looks for control over her own life.

In an attempt to answer her needs in a roundabout way, of nourishing herself, finding worth and appreciation, and having control over her own life, the woman turns to food. Her overeating expresses her neediness and desires; these she tries to control by dieting. The problem, though, is that this kind of control is something she develops 'outside' herself – something out there, rather than something emanating from within herself. She uses devices such as scales to weigh herself and dictate the amount of food she takes in, or diet sheets to dictate what she can and cannot eat, what is 'allowed' and how many calories she is permitted to swallow. She also uses a watch to tell her if she is allowed to feel hungry, according to what time it is. If so many hours have passed since her last meal, she must eat so much now. If she is hungry before then, she is not to eat until a sensible interval has elapsed. If she was 'good' yesterday and ate according to the diet sheet or ate fewer calories, then she deserves something forbidden today. Or if she is going to go on a crash diet tomorrow and is about to lose most of her excess weight, then she can have a binge today. This way of controlling her life not only brings about order and gives her the safety of a day-to-day organized routine, but it can also become very regimented and restrictive.

The anorexic's control over herself is relentless. By rigorously restricting her food intake, she attempts to control all her physical and emotional appetites. Nothing escapes this tight control, nothing is supposed to be assimilated except under strict rules. There are no compromises. Whenever the control slips, an enormous flood of emotions of guilt, self-hatred, blame and self-disgust come up. Tight control, in addition to its 'positive' results of staying thin, also brings a feeling of being relaxed and comfortable within the well-known sphere of the routine of ordinary life.

Many people use self-control or self-denial to make themselves feel better. In all the major religions we find a strand of asceticism in which there is an attempt to subdue and overcome an unwanted part of the self. There is a powerful and not completely conscious feeling within most of us that the body is 'bad' and that by subduing, controlling or neglecting it, we can become 'better' people. In the anorexic, this feeling becomes very dominant. Her need to control her body becomes a moral obsession. As she gets thinner and thinner, she experiences herself as getting better and better. This, of course, is why the symptom is so difficult to give up.

Cultural and social attitudes to women's bodies

Kim Chernin, in her book *Womansize*, attempts to explain the obsession society has with woman's body:

> Our preoccupation with it derives from the first moments and hours and years of life. And we understand also how our troubles over the body are even older than our first struggle to control it and how this first grief about the body must have been learned in a woman's arms and at our mother's breast. This first experience when we are held, awakens a sea of sensations, sight not clearly distinguished from touch or feel or sounds. Inner and outer not separated from one another. Like a tropical paradise where food comes magically when needed. It is a time of life in which woman is the universe, her body our source of life and comfort, our feeding and touching and feeling and seeing and sensing reaching out and finding, knowing, all spin round the softness and roundness of a woman's body.[4]

Dorothy Dinnerstein[5] writes that one basis for our species' fundamental ambivalence towards its female members lies in the fact that the early mother is a source of ultimate distress as well as ultimate joy. She is both nourishing and disappointing, both alluring and threatening. She is the source of food, warmth, comfort and entertainment. But the baby, no matter how well it is cared for, suffers some hunger or cold, some belly-aches or unpleasant noise or movement, some loneliness or boredom, and how is it to know that she is not the source of all these things too?

And, of course, often the mother herself *is* a source of frustration, pain, anger, disappointment and many other mixed feelings. For both men and women, for all of us, the first and most powerful influence and source of mixed feelings is a woman's body. It is no surprise, then, that the woman's body becomes the symbol for so many fantasies, for so many feelings, that it is a symbol of fertility as well as powerlessness, of love as well as anxiety, of helplessness as well as control, of dependence as well as fear. It makes sense, then, that so much is invested in women's bodies.

The whole advertising industry, fashion, film, food and diet industries, centre around woman's body and woman's sexuality. Advertisements for a chocolate bar, a soap, an aeroplane, a car, a perfume or even British Rail all use women's bodies, usually naked or half-naked, with insinuations (and often more than just insinuations) about their sexuality.

It is always women's bodies and fashion that are at the centre of changes in society. Susie Orbach in *Hunger Strike* reminds us of the way images of femininity have changed from Marilyn Monroe to Twiggy, and how current images are of little girls rather than of women with feminine characteristics.[6] Many of the photographic models of today are in fact children no more than nine or ten years old, dressed up in women's clothes and communicating to women that somehow we ought to be able to look like them! The advertisers of those fashionable jeans that allow no space for a woman's hips actually use adolescent boys, masquerading as women, to sell their product to women. No wonder that women are left feeling they never look quite as good as the pictures.

Kim Chernin[7] suggests that the more powerful women become, the more society demands images of powerlessness in the way women are presented. Successful women in important positions are encouraged to look like thin little girls who have no connection with the powerful women they are inside. The more influence women have on all fronts, the more powerful they are in real terms, the thinner, weaker, girlier the fashion industry demands them to become.

At any moment in history, the image of the beautiful or even acceptable female body is limited to a very few body types. Those women who conform to these projected images are acknowledged as the beauties of their time. The actual reality is such that if you look at women's bodies, no one body looks like another. There are as many body types as there are bodies. And yet there is always one type that is more acceptable at any given time, and women have to comply with that type; if they do not, they must experience both personally and publicly the humiliation, pain, shame and embarrassment of being not just different but inferior. This does not leave room for any uniqueness or variation in women's appearance.

Women are expected to conform to a certain body type and

if they do not do this naturally, which is the case for most women in real life, they should do something about it; they should learn to control their body in some way or another to fit that expectation. Our society makes the extraordinary assumption that women's bodies are infinitely changeable. Magazines tell us that hips are 'in' this year, or large breasts are 'out'. They are encouraging women to believe that they have not only the ability but also the obligation to change and conform.

What relationship does a woman have to her body? Her body is looked at by men, by other women and by herself. Men are supposed to look, admire, whistle and comment, and they may do that at any given time while she is walking the street. Her body is on constant display; it is like public property, available for anyone to at least comment on, if not pinch or touch. This attention is not always favourable. Fat women, together with black women, constantly find themselves the recipients of disparaging comments and abuse because they do not conform to particular stereotypes in appearance.

A woman is primarily the one who must be beautiful in order to be chosen by a man. She is the one who is waiting – pretty, well-dressed and made up – for the man who is supposed to make the first active move towards her, *depending on her looks*. This 'active-man-looks/passive-woman-looked-at' is the determining factor in how men and women are perceived and perceive themselves. Women enter beauty contests in which they stand, almost naked, for people to judge their appearance, and their rewards for winning are prizes, fame, money and admiration. In many cases a woman's appearance determines her social activities, and, at times, it dictates whether she will be accepted for a certain job, even for one that does not necessarily require beauty. As Susie Orbach writes in *Fat is a Feminist Issue*:

> This emphasis on presentation as the central aspect of a woman's existence makes her extremely self-conscious. It demands that she occupies herself with a self-image that others will find pleasing and attractive, an image that will immediately convey what kind of woman she is. She must observe and evaluate herself, scrutinizing every detail of herself as though she were an outside judge. She attempts to make herself in the image of womanhood presented by billboards, newspapers, magazines and television . . . Since women are taught to see themselves from the outside as candidates for men, they become prey to the huge fashion

and diet industries that first set up the ideal image and then exhort women to meet it. The message is loud and clear – the woman's body is not her own. The woman's body is not satisfactory as it is.[8]

Thus women do not look at themselves with their own inner vision, but are trying to evaluate their bodies according to an image presented in the media, according to some idea set up for them by society.

The emphasis put on external appearance not only forces a woman to look at herself through others' eyes, but also to look at her body as the main attribute of her personality. When looking in the mirror a woman looks for her essential quality, her identity, her self. Obviously these ideal media images are unattainable for most women and hence most women will never be satisfied with the way they look. There will always be something that is not quite right. As one woman wrote in her letter to us, 'I always loathed my body. Even when I was slim I hated it. Fat or thin, I always felt there was something wrong with my body.'

Even though they are constantly concentrating on how they look and on their bodies, women are nevertheless mostly out of touch with them. This is expressed in an extreme way by anorexics and compulsive eaters. The overweight woman as well as the anorexic is distanced from the fact that she has a body. Her body image is distorted to the point that she does not acknowledge her body as hers – she disowns her own body.

Both the compulsive eater and the anorexic disembody themselves by living in their heads. To both, the body is a burden they have to carry, a trap, an enemy. They punish themselves and others through their bodies; they manipulate their bodies in order to say things for them, to give messages. When a compulsive eater describes a binge, she often expresses it in terms of being split in two: one half of her is eating without control, violently, painfully, not knowing why, how much or what she is stuffing down, and the other half is watching, loathing, hating and despairing. The compulsive eater and the anorexic share the feeling that their spirit is a prisoner in the cage of their body.

Through her looks – the woman is promised – she will get a man, a family, achieve happiness. This way of seeing our body as an attribute, a commodity through which we get the 'good' things in life, is what makes both women and men see women's bodies as 'objects' and what makes women so out of touch with their bodies. The woman sees it as something separate from 'her' which she can manipulate. She can control and change it at will according to the prevailing fashion. It is not only her clothes which should change to 'fit the bill' but also her hairstyle, the shape of her body, its smell – and the stereotypes vary over time. Nowadays thin is 'in'. Watching films from past years shows how ideals of attractiveness change in a relatively short period of time.

Models these days are becoming thinner and thinner, and this trend is affecting girls at earlier and earlier ages. As early as eight or nine years old, girls begin to watch what they are eating in an attempt to take control over a body which is beginning to mature, to change shape.

It is important to understand that this preference for thinness and the fear and loathing of the bodies of mature women has a meaning. It can be seen as an attempt to get rid of the unacceptable and unwanted aspects of femininity, leaving only a palatable and non-threatening version of woman.

In mythological representations of women this split shows itself in the creation of two kinds of woman – the mother and the whore. (In the Christian tradition this is exemplified by the two Marys – the Virgin Mary and Mary Magdalen.)

The whore is sexual, wild, full of desires, dangerous, with her seduction which can drive a man crazy or to his death (in many mythological stories the man goes to war or does irrational deeds just because he has been seduced by a woman; Adam and Eve lost the garden of Eden because of her seduction). She is dirty, manipulative and will stop at nothing to get what she wants – usually a man's heart and his property or kingdom. The mother is quite her opposite – she is pure, loving, innocent, sacrificing, nourishing, non-sexual, clean, wants nothing for herself but to devote herself to her man and her children. She is holy and completely good.

Adrianne Rich, in *Of Woman Born*, says:

This same body with its bleeding and its mysteries is her single destiny and justification in life. These two ideals have been deeply internalized by women even in the most independent of us, those of us who seem to lead the freest of lives. In order to maintain two such notions each in its contradictory purity, the masculine imagination has had to divide to see us and force us to see ourselves as polarized into good and evil, fertile and barren, pure or impure and all these fantasies are symbolized in and centred around a woman's body.⁹

Is it any surprise, then, that it is the woman's body – the body that carries such entirely conflicting and contradictory meanings – which becomes the arena within which women unconsciously choose to express the conflicts in their lives?

NOTES

1 P. Schilder (1935): *The Image and Appearance of the Human Body*, Psyche Monographs, 4, London.

2 P. Shuttle and P. Redgrove (1978): *The Wise Wound*, Penguin, Harmondsworth.

3 M. Woodman (1980). *The Owl Was a Baker's Daughter. Obesity, Anorexia Nervosa and the Repressed Feminine*, Inner City Books, Canada.

4 K. Chernin (1981): *Womansize. The Tyranny of Slenderness*, The Women's Press, London.

5 D. Dinnerstein (1987); *The Rocking of the Cradle and the Ruling of the World*, The Women's Press, London.

6 S. Orbach (1986): *Hunger Strike*, Faber, London.

7 K. Chernin, ibid.

8 S. Orbach (1978): *Fat is a Feminist Issue*, Hamlyn, London.

9 A. Rich (1977): *Of Woman Born*, Virago, London.

6
WOMEN'S PSYCHOLOGY

The psychology of eating disorders

In the previous chapter we looked at the way in which social pressures and processes shape women's relationship to food and their feelings about their own bodies. In this chapter we consider how women's development within the family and in particular within the mother/daughter relationship makes women vulnerable to eating disorders. We shall be describing the feelings which underlie eating disorders, feelings which so many women want to split off and deny.

In order more fully to address the question of why so many women and relatively so few men suffer from eating disorders, we have to begin to understand the meaning of eating and how this might be different for women and men.

If we consider the earliest experience which human beings have of eating, of being fed, we go back at once to the first days and weeks of life, in which baby and mother are all-important and in which the baby has no existence outside that relationship. The most important element within that very early relationship is the infant's need for food and the ability of the mother to supply it. This remains true whether the mother feeds her baby with breast or bottle, and indeed whether it is the biological mother or some other mother-substitute who cares for the baby. In these very early days of life, when both baby and mother feel a sense of unity, of oneness, of not being separate, feeding is the activity which embodies (for the baby) and symbolizes (for the mother) this relationship. Feeding, at the beginning of all our lives, is not merely about physical nourishment. It is, of course, feeding which keeps the baby physically alive, but in addition, it is the relationship with the mother which ensures its emotional survival. It is through the act of feeding that the baby experiences all the detailed caring and concern upon which it is so dependent. Winnicott describes infant feeding as 'a putting into practice of a love relationship between two human beings'.[1]

The importance of this, from our point of view, is that our earliest experience of feeding is one in which we experience total dependence and in which, if all goes well, our emotional as well as our physical needs are met. Gradually, as the baby grows and begins to understand the world of other people, it begins to recognize the difference between the need for food and the need for caring. Some parents, of course, make this recognition more difficult by continuing to try to meet emotional needs with food. The mother who offers her child a sweet when she is upset is encouraging her to revert back to a time when comfort, love, holding and milk were all one.

All of us, whatever happens to us in our lives, retain a sense of this link between feeding and the meeting of emotional need. Quite unconsciously, when we feel particularly needy emotionally, this will have a connection for us with physical nourishment. Many people, when they are upset or unhappy, find themselves putting their hand in the biscuit tin. When we become especially depressed, this will very often have an effect on our food intake. Either we will try to comfort ourselves with food or else we will reject such comfort altogether and lose our appetite. Given this link between eating and the meeting of emotional need, we can say with some confidence that someone who develops an eating disorder has a particular difficulty with identifying, accepting and meeting their emotional needs.

Needs

According to Jean Baker Miller:

> Women have been led to feel that they can integrate and use all their attributes if they use them for others but not for themselves. They have developed the sense that their lives should be guided by the constant need to attune themselves to the wishes, desires and needs of others ... The ego, the 'I' of psychoanalysis, may not be at all appropriate when talking about women. Women have different organizing principles around which their psyches are structured. One of these principles is that they exist to serve other people's needs ... first men and later children ... as if they did not have needs of their own, as if one could serve others without simultaneously attending to one's own interest and desires ...[2]

Fighting Food

Thus a 'real' woman is someone who doesn't ask openly and overtly for what she needs or wants. This situation has important consequences for women:

(a) Many women cannot tolerate the thought or even allow themselves to feel that their life activities are for themselves.
(b) Some women try to meet their needs vicariously, by looking after other people.
(c) Women believe that their own needs, even though unexamined, untested, and unexpressed, will somehow be fulfilled in return for serving others, and that they will be loved because of their services.

Most importantly, women feel that their needs are dirty, unacceptable and overwhelming. They feel that they should not have needs, let alone express them or expect them to be met. If they do have needs, these must be bad and come from an unwanted aspect of their personality, unacceptable to themselves or others. If they express a need, this means they are weak, and once they begin to be in touch with this part of themselves, all their needs will come bursting through and will destroy everything and everyone in sight. So it is better to ignore the whole area of their own needs and not to acknowledge its existence or even try to express it.

Anorexics, bulimics and compulsive eaters express this in a very clear way. Since women feel that their own needs are unacceptable, they have to find ways of dealing with such unwanted entities inside themselves. As most women find dealing directly with this conflict very difficult, the answer will be either to substitute some compensation for the meeting of these needs, or to pretend that the needs are not there at all, thus creating a person who is totally convinced she has no needs whatsoever. For the anorexic, this extends even to denying her need for the basic function of eating. So the anorexic unconsciously makes the statement: 'I have so many needs that they will be overwhelming to anybody even to know about them. I am so scared by this that I cut off all needs and make the overt statement: "I do not need anything."'

The compulsive eater unconsciously feels the same – that she would overwhelm anyone with her needs – so she has to find some other way of meeting them. The most immediate way is, every time the need arises, to use food to shut it down, to cut it off, to bring back relaxation and pretend that the need does not exist any longer.

For the bulimic woman, when a need is aroused of any kind, food is taken in, consumed in huge quantities, or even 'ordinary' quantities, but when that need has to be acknowledged it is so terrifying that it immediately has to be negated. This is done symbolically by vomiting the food which was consumed as an answer to the initial need and which in some way also represents the need. Symbolically negating the need and its acknowledgement is done by throwing it up.

In all these problems the woman first turns to the idea of food whenever a need or a conflict about needs is aroused. The behaviour, however, is different in each case: the anorexic will prevent herself from eating, the compulsive eater will eat and keep the food in while experiencing self-hate, guilt and regret, and the bulimic will eat and will act on these feelings to push the food out again, to undo the 'awful' deed.

Mother–daughter relationships

In the previous chapter we looked at the ways in which mothers may unconsciously pass on to their daughters their own anxieties and sense of unease about their bodies. The difficulty which so many women experience in identifying and expressing their own needs also has its origin in the early relationship a little girl has with her mother.

Even before a baby is born, its parents have feelings and ideas about what that child will be like. In spite of modern notions of equality, the birth of a son is, at least unconsciously, regarded as a very special event. It is he who will transmit the family's name and, among certain social groups, inherit the family's fortune. In some societies, the birth of a son is celebrated with a big party and a girl's with a simple greeting.

On the other hand, the birth of a girl means something special too. The mother is likely to see in her baby daughter someone who will be like her and who will take care of her. The mother's sense of identification with her baby daughter has some important consequences. A mother may have a particularly clear intuitive understanding of her baby daughter's needs at the very beginning. She is much more likely to try to understand the baby girl from within herself, rather than seeing her as someone separate from herself whom she has to get to know.

The negative side of this identification is that the mother sees in her daughter someone who will be like herself, who will look after others and will not have needs herself. The sight of her daughter's neediness is likely to awaken in the mother the painful feelings associated with her own unmet needs. Many mothers find it difficult to respond fully to their daughter's needs; it is difficult for a mother to give to her daughter what she has never been fully given herself. The little girl learns not only that it is better to meet others' needs than to make demands herself, but also that her own needs are bad and unacceptable. They upset her mother, and anyway, being demanding is not the way to get what she needs. She should not remind her mother of the very painful state she herself is in – the deprivation is which she is caught – so that her mother will not have to identify with these unpleasant emotions.

Eichenbaum and Orbach, in *Understanding Women*,[3] suggest that this dynamic produces a kind of pull–push effect in the mother–daughter relationship. The mother wants her daughter to stay close, but when she comes close, mother gives her cues which tell her she should be less needy, less demanding and really should be able to take care of herself. The period of symbiosis between mother and baby daughter, in which the baby remains merged with the mother and totally dependent on her, is prematurely curtailed. This means that women very often grow up with the sense that their need for dependence has never really been met. In spite of this rather unfulfilling state of affairs, mother and daughter remain close. The developing daughter is not encouraged to be independent or to break away from her mother in a healthy and satisfying way. She stays close, but feels unsatisfied. Hilde Bruch[4] points out that mothers sometimes anticipate their babies' needs in a way which can be unhelpful. She suggests that anorexia can sometimes have its origins in the earliest relationship between mother and daughter. The mother, through her identification with the baby, will tend to feed the baby when she 'knows', or thinks she knows, the baby is hungry. Rather than waiting for some sign from the baby, like crying, which indicates hunger, she preempts the gesture and offers food. Not only does this dynamic keep the baby close and completely dependent on the mother, it also prevents the baby from developing any sense of her own autonomy. She fails to learn to distinguish needs and feelings which originate within herself from 'care' which is imposed from the outside.

If this situation continues, the child will grow up with a sense that being nurtured is a way of pleasing mother, with little relation to its own actual needs or feelings. Any expression of need which does emanate from the child herself may well make the mother feel anxious and guilty, as though she should have known about the need and met it before it ever arose. The child, in turn, learns not to do this, not to upset the mother, but to take whatever mother offers when she offers it.

Such a child will certainly appear well cared for, and quite possibly happy as well. But something essential is missing. The child does not have the opportunity to develop a sense of autonomy, of being an active person in the world with thoughts, feelings, needs and demands.

From a developmental point of view, the crucial point in the mother–daughter relationship comes from this picture. Immediately after the birth the mother may have a few weeks of feeling immense loneliness, isolation and misery, as well as quite different feelings of excitement, pride and happiness. When looking at her baby boy from this painful space she might try to make him a substitute for a missing husband, absent at work or elsewhere. When looking at a baby girl, however, there is the overwhelmingly painful realization that this child is going to feel the same one day – isolated and lonely.

In one of our workshops, Wendy talked about her two-year-old son; when he comes to her to ask for hugs she somehow always wants to hug him, always feels he is wanted and lovely. However, when her four-year-old daughter needs a hug, Wendy has quite a different emotional response. She usually feels she is too tired, she is too busy or she just doesn't feel like hugging at the moment. In a role play, in which one of the therapists played the daughter, what emerged was the pain, hatred and disgust that arise in Wendy towards her daughter's needs. We then asked her to role-play herself as a little girl while one of us was her mother – withholding, too busy: 'I don't have time for your needy emotional scenes.' When she changed again into being the 'good mother', the one who is giving and loving and caring, Wendy burst into tears.

She felt that it was just as painful to have love and care as not to have it because it reminded her of all she never had.

Very soon the little girl is going to be sent away from her mother, to be 'separate', in order to learn how to be a good mother herself and to take care of her father and siblings (playing with dolls is one reflection of this).

Many of the issues which arise for girls in the mother–daughter relationship are expressed through eating disorders. It often seems almost as though the food, which is such a problem for the woman, a source of very powerful conflicting feelings, represents the mother in some sense.

Often the compulsive eater has been force-fed as a child or cajoled into eating when she was not hungry. In many cases her mother has put all her own identity into the food, and if the girl does not eat the food, the mother is not a good mother; her sense of identity suffers. The mother loves her daughter but finds no other way of expressing this except through food. In the same way, if the daughter rejects the food it means she doesn't love her mother.

Often when the daughter falls down or gets angry or cries she is given a sweet, as if a sweet is the ultimate comfort for every uncomfortable feeling (for both mother and girl). So the girl learns that food is comforting and is also a way to express love and care and to accept or reject the mother and her love.

The woman in an anorexic phase very often re-experiences all the ambivalence she felt towards her mother in infancy. She will sometimes alternate between feeling totally dependent on her mother for everything, especially for her mother to feed her – and at the same time wanting to angrily push everyone away, especially her mother, in an assertion of independence.

The anorexia, then, becomes a total rejection of what the mother represents. It becomes the ultimate statement of self and separateness from the mother and all her behaviour. The statement says: 'There is one area where you cannot force your opinion or impose your ways on me – my eating. I reject you and your food. I am "me" and totally separate from you. I will not give you even the basic pleasure of feeding me.' The other half of the message is: 'I cannot manage without you. I cannot do anything for myself. I cannot even feed myself. Look at me. Without you, I will die.'

For the bulimic woman, the situation seems somewhat

more complicated. Her relationship with food shows some of the ambivalence present in her relationship with her mother. She did not experience her mother as completely rejecting or accepting. Her symptom suggests that she was painfully in touch with how much she needed her mother but that this need was a source of great guilt and shame. From feeling that she will have what she needs and in abundance, she swings into a frantic attempt to be free of such feelings. Her sense of safety truly lies in her emptiness and self-sufficiency. Mother, her promised care and concern, are all angrily vomited up, expressing her rage and disappointment for what she cannot have.

Father–daughter relationships

We have described the relationship between mother and daughter as one which is characterized by bonding, symbiosis and a sense of oneness. The father is important to the girl's development in terms of her attempts to get out of this merged state, to separate from her mother.

The father is likely to be the first 'other' that the girl comes to know. He is different from both herself and her mother and he can relate to her from outside of that symbiotic bond. He is the one who can potentially help her in defining and developing her separate self as an individual woman, different from her mother.

The daughter needs her father to affirm her sexuality and femininity. She needs him to appreciate her sexuality and attractiveness without acting it out, without himself being a sexual man with her.

The other very important role of the father is to model for the daughter a being-in-the-world as opposed to being-in-relationship (or being-in-the-home) which is the model she will take from her mother. It is from her father that the girl will learn the confidence and competence to operate in a world which is competitive, unsupportive and at times hostile and full of conflicts – in short, a world which operates primarily according to masculine principles.

The father also symbolizes for the daughter authority and law. Providing the father's authority is not too rigid, it is by her identification with him that she will learn to accept authority and also to find her own inner sense of authority, limits and boundaries.

Jessica Benjamin,[5] in her study of women's identity and the father–daughter relationship, describes both the needs of the growing girl and some of the things which can go wrong. She points to the way in which the little girl as a toddler shows considerable interest in her father and in particular in his body, his penis, his maleness – the obvious way in which he is different from her mother and herself. Benjamin believes that little girls, like little boys, seek to identify with their fathers. The girl cannot identify with the father in a literal way, as the boy does, by being the same. Instead, she looks for a relationship in which her uniqueness will be recognized and affirmed. However, the father's need to assert his difference from women, from his mother and his wife, may prevent him from being able to give the girl what she needs.

While the father may be able to relate to her as 'sweet', as a nascent sexual object, he may find it more difficult to accept her identity and in particular her need to use him as a way out of her relationship with her mother and into the outside world. If the father fails to 'recognize' his daughter, his withdrawal from her will push her back into her closeness with her mother.

In this situation, femininity, sexuality, the possession of a woman's body, can become a source of humiliation, failure and shame. The girl finds herself struggling against her father and his power over and contempt for women. At the same time, she would like to be like him. Very often, the girl sees her parents' relationship as one of inequality, in which her father does not really value and respect her mother as a person in her own right. She therefore cannot use him to help her gain a sense of her own identity.

Many women who develop eating disorders are struggling to find and discover this sense of autonomy and selfhood. They are stuck in a stultifying dependence on mother and cannot use a helpful identification with father to change things, to become separate. If the parents are not able to be secure in their difference from each other, if difference implies conflict, inequality and guilt, then identification with either parent will cause tremendous problems in relation to the woman's own identity.

We often find that women who go on to develop bulimia have come from families where there have been divorces or separations. They have very often been separated from their fathers and out of a sense of rejection, as well as loyalty to mother, have been unable to make any positive identification with him. They thus end up with the familiar split between the successful coping person they present to the world and the despised sense of femininity and sexuality which it conceals.

Women who develop anorexia have frequently been clever and talented children who have not been able to integrate this competence (which can be thought of as a 'male' quality) with femininity. They feel unable to separate from mother and take their talents out of the family and into the world. Whatever has gone wrong for the anorexic – and innate factors of character certainly play a part – she has been unable to use her father in a positive way to separate from mother and find her identity as a woman in her own right.

Dependence

For the little boy, independence is highly valued and is encouraged. For little girls, however, the most important thing to learn is to do things for others, to learn how to serve and care. All too often, girls do not experience the process of working through their dependent stage into a 'healthy' sense of self and separateness from their mother. Instead they feel prematurely pushed away from mother into a 'good little girl' role. They are not independent or separate but are going through an artificial independence in which they play a role they are not yet ready for – a 'doll's game' that the family structure encourages.

On the one hand the girl is kept unseparated from mother and on the other she is artificially pushed away. She has to be Daddy's sweet little girl and act in a 'feminine' way to get his attention and appreciation. What makes it even more difficult is that she is the same as mother physically, so she cannot even use this as a source of feeling different or 'separate'. She is 'the same' as mother, yet is not allowed to work through that 'sameness' into a clear sense of two separate people. Long before working through that, she has already acquired another pseudo-independent role, having others depend on her. The implications of this situation are fully discussed by Sheila Ernst[6] in her most appropriately titled paper, 'Can a Daughter be a Woman?'

From this picture one can easily understand the very negative feelings which become attached to being dependent. Dependence becomes associated with weakness, low self-image, worthlessness and self-hate. Frustration then inevitably follows in a society that, by definition, dictates women's financial dependence (and all the other dependences that this entails) on men within the conventional nuclear family. Passivity and receptivity are other attributes connected with dependence – waiting for things to happen rather than making them occur, not asserting what one wants but waiting for it to be given. The anger, confusion and frustration when they don't come are also repressed, as dependence does not permit such emotions to be expressed. For generations, in countless situations, women have had to say 'yes' when they felt 'no'; or they might not even have permitted themselves to feel the 'no', because saying 'no' might mean having no means of material or financial support.

Add to that situation the development of the little girl: the role she is encouraged to adopt is that of the 'little mother'. A daughter is pushed to act a mature and adult role. She may be expected to mother younger children, but when she does she is not given respect or the rights of authority, autonomy and decision-making that such a role should entail. In her actions, therefore, she is mature, but not in the way she is led to feel – and does feel – about herself. She is in fact still a little girl, dependent on her parents' instructions, 'indulging' in the activities of mature and adult people.

This little girl, who still feels like a little girl inside, who had to mother before she ever had a chance to sort out her own dependence, will always exist in the grown-up woman. The discrepancies and conflicts this creates will continue into her adult life. There will always be the wish to be consumed and submerged into relationships with others, together with the knowledge that this kind of symbiosis is a fantasy and will lead to yet another disappointment. There is also the obligation to take care of others when the wish is to be taken care of.

In the light of all this, it is not surprising, therefore, that women need to find ways to transpose this humiliating dependence. Women express these conflicts in many ways, often producing disabling symptoms. Agoraphobia, for example, can be understood as a solution to the conflict between dependence and independence expressed in the fear of going out, the fear of self-assertion and independence. Eating disorders are other symptoms which express this conflict.

These are, of course, extreme individual ways of dealing with the conflict, but the structure of conventional partriarchal society leaves little room for women to express them in more direct ways. To shift from indirect to direct means involves a long re-learning process and hard work.

Both anorexia and bulimia have to be understood as responses to conflicts about dependence. For the anorexic woman the need for food, the obsession with it, the dependence on it as well as dependence on other people, are totally and utterly cut off. She is not dependent on anyone or anything. She is obsessed with, and hence dependent on, the rigorous rules by which she runs her life. She is dependent on the shop (usually the same one) where she buys the minute amount of food she allows herself to eat; she is obsessed with – and hence dependent on – her weight, the scales, the knowledge that she has lost another 100g since yesterday. She is dependent on the long, exhausting walks that she forces herself to go on in order to burn off the few calories she has consumed during the day. It is as if she is hanging on to the framework and regimented structure of her life in order to keep herself going and needs no substance in terms of nurturance.

The bulimic woman treats her dependence on food or on any other nourishment with the same violence but perhaps more ambivalence: there is an immense need, an immense dependence on it, yet she immediately rejects it. The bulimic woman recognizes her dependence on food but cannot accept it and will therefore not let any of the food stay in.

Susan, a participant in one of the anorexia groups at the Women's Therapy Centre, used to come religiously to every session of the group, but always arrived a few minutes late, after the group had already started. She would apologize and mention how important the group was for her. Her way of not putting on weight was to chew her food but not swallow it and to spit it out into a bag. She did not reveal this, however, until the last session, whereupon she became the centre of attention. The women were angry as well as supportive towards her. They wanted to help, but why had she waited until now to tell the group about her problem? Each woman said some things that were important in terms of the relationship between her and the group and her relationship with the individuals in it. To every remark, before the woman had even finished her sentence, Susan had an answer unrelated to what had been said. It was clear that she needed the group's feedback and support, but it was just as clear that she could not take it in. She was spitting out any piece of nourishment she was given.

The most painful aspect of this situation for most women is being tormented by the immense desire for and dependence on nourishment and the constant hope of getting it, while at the same time being totally unable to take it in or keep it in. Another bulimic woman once told us that her only way of feeling alive was through vomiting – the convulsion of the body and face that she experienced, the tears and sounds and energy of the stomach and the body as a whole, were for her the only expression of her aliveness. The rejection of the nourishment needed to sustain life (food) was her way of being alive. This shows how negatively the dependence on nourishment is seen, in that such extreme action is needed to deny and reject it.

For the compulsive eater the picture is slightly different. The feelings of dependence and the need for people, and the fear of these feelings, are transformed into dependence on food. As for the anorexic, there is the terror of expressing dependence on people who are in the end always disappointing and who can never really meet these needs. Women are supposed to take care of others through food. The compulsive eater finds that she can also take care of herself through food, but because there are so many other emotions involved, such as guilt, anger and self-hatred, she constantly needs to 'take care' of herself (with food) in order to make herself forget all her other needs. Time and again, women in groups are heard to say: 'Food never disappoints me. It is always there, never turns its back on me, never humiliates, hurts or betrays me.' What better object for dependence?

For the compulsive eater, the dependence issue is twofold. A woman becomes overweight in order to divert her attention from her overwhelming dependence needs, but at the same time there are other people from the outside – husband, mother, children, etc. – expressing their dependence on her. In order to keep all these demands out and leave some space for herself, she creates a physical space within her body, protected by her fat, which keeps the demands at bay. For the compulsive eater, bulimic and anorexic, the disorder itself is a way of expressing a self – of saying to others: 'I am not dependent on you, I am not weak and vulnerable to you, I am independent. I have my obsession, my food, my friend.'

Sexuality

The issue of sexuality encapsulates many of the themes already discussed in this chapter and the previous one in relation to women's condition and conditioning in our society. It is a complex issue. If we look at our mothers' generation, women then were expected not to have sexual urges, and not to be involved in any sexual relationships before actually getting married. Virginity as a symbol of not having been with any other man was a very important asset for a woman in order to be fit to marry. Women now in their thirties and forties experienced this when they were growing up. The younger generation have externally had a different experience, in being allowed or even expected to have several lovers, and to engage in free sexual interactions. Sexuality no longer has to be hidden or 'saved' for a very special relationship. Women can have a variety of sexual partners. Yet our social reality is such that in advertisements on TV, woman's body is still used as a sexual object, still the focus of a cultural obsession with appearance and with thinness. Still there are very limited ways a woman can look if she wants to conform to society's view of what is sexual and acceptable.

Phyllis Chesler writes in *Women and Madness*:

> Women can never be sexually actualized as long as men control the means of production and reproduction. Women have had to barter their sexuality for economic survival and maternity . . . They have been seen as not really 'needing' orgasms as much as they need love, maternity and fine silverware . . . Women are sexually repressed by patriarchal institutions which enforce fear, dislike and confusion about the female sexual and reproductive anatomy in both men and women.[7]

Mothers are often unable to help their daughters to feel good about their sexuality. Mothers and daughters alike are subject to similar attitudes, where women's bodies are at the same time objects of pride and shame, adored and feared. Girls do *not* learn to like or be proud of their bodies, which makes sexuality even more complicated than it is already. Mothers convey to daughters their shame and dislike of their own bodies as well. They often convey their disapproval of freedom in sexuality and are very secretive, which means girls are often left ignorant.

Fighting Food

Embarrassment and shame are common feelings. Growing up with this set of beliefs and feelings, a girl goes out into the world and experiences the humiliation of being made a sex object. As Jean Baker Miller writes:

> When one is an object, not a subject, all of one's own physical and sexual impulses and interests are presumed not to exist independently. They are to be brought into existence only by and for others – controlled, defined and used.[8]

A woman is to be passive and not initiate sexual encounters. She is only a reactor and must wait. She is allowed to have sexual feelings only in response to a man, to whom she surrenders.

One way to cope with this (indirectly) is for the girl to try to desexualize herself. Eating problems, which are usually accompanied by a low self-image and an especially low body-image, serve as such attempts.

For the compulsive eater there are two levels on which this operates. One is eating and the other is becoming overweight. Whenever sexual feelings arise in her which are very threatening or when someone makes sexual advances towards her, the way to cut off these feelings is by eating, thus stuffing down unacceptable and uncomfortable feelings. The second level is based on the assumption that fat women are unattractive, not feminine and even non-sexual.

The anorexic woman, by having just the opposite body – thin or skinny – also considers herself asexual. Her attempts at self-starvation are an attempt to become thin to the point of being desexualized in appearance and, by the loss of her periods, desexualized physiologically too.

Many bulimic women appear on the surface as sexually 'liberated' women, women who can manage their own sexuality, but underneath is all the uncertainty, the feeling of being judged and many of the 'old-fashioned' feelings of shame and self-disgust. Often their experience is encapsulated in the thought: 'How can I kiss someone with the mouth I have just vomited from?' Many women we have worked with said that they felt there was something very wrong, very bad about their sexuality, their sexual desires, and many felt it was a representation of the messy, uncontrolled part of themselves that should not be allowed to be seen.

NOTES

1 D. W. Winnicott (1964): *The Child, The Family and the Outside World*, Penguin, Harmondsworth.

2 J. Baker Miller (1976): *Toward a New Psychology of Women*, Penguin, Harmondsworth.

3 L. Eichenbaum and S. Orbach (1983): *Understanding Women*, Penguin, London.

4 H. Bruch (1974): *Eating Disorders*, Routledge & Kegan Paul, London.

5 J. Benjamin (1988): *The Bonds of Love*, Pantheon Books, New York.

6 S. Ernst and M. Maguire (1987): *Living with the Sphinx*, The Women's Press, London.

7 P. Chesler (1974): *Women and Madness*, Allen Lane, London.

8 J. Baker Miller, ibid.

7
BOUNDARY AND SELF

In this chapter we introduce two psychological concepts which have particular relevance to eating disorders. These are the concepts of 'self' and 'boundary', and they are closely linked together. First we will briefly describe what each of them means and offer some theoretical definitions of the concepts and the connections between them. Next we will discuss some of the issues which are related and relevant to women's boundaries and expression of self. Finally, we will look at how these concepts relate specifically to eating problems and their significance for therapy.

A very simple explanation of the concept of boundaries is knowing who you are, where you end and where the 'other' begins. This raises questions of what your limits are, how far you will let people come into your own space (or you go into theirs), what is private and not to be shared, and what is public. What is central and what is peripheral to that space? What are your needs, wants, desires, beliefs and values? Who and what is allowed in and to what extent (saying yes and no)? What are the criteria according to which you allow people, things and beliefs to come in (and are allowed to go out into another's space), and how do these criteria operate?

The idea of choice is most important in relation to this concept. To what extent is one capable of selecting how to use one's time and space (be it one's home, body, or money) in a way which will fit with one's needs, wishes and responsibilities? There is a process of constant negotiation within oneself in relation to this selection process.

To understand this concept it may help to imagine a house which is yours with a fence around it. The house represents you and the fence around it your boundaries – is the fence so high and thick that no one but you can be seen? Or is it so low and thin that everything and everyone can look inside? Is it a tightly closed fence that does not allow any room for anyone or anything to happen? Or is it so widely open and unguarded that everyone can come in at any time without notice? The process of selection and discrimination, taking into account our own feelings, needs, wishes and responsibilities, is what creates our sense of boundaries.

By the 'expression of self' we mean the ability to express the central core of the personality, the self, creatively and with self-respect. It implies an appreciation for that centre from which one's actions and feelings originate, and expressing this through activity. This, of course, is an idealistic picture; it is the essence of maturity and psychological well-being. In fact people are on a continuum leading to this position, and some people more than others will operate from their centre and 'real self', not out of external prohibitions, fear or guilt. Of course, in order to have and keep social order people must understand and accept some rules of society and accept responsibility and authority, but this is the constant process of negotiation which goes on – not blindly accepting everything or blindly going against everything, and especially not acting simply out of fear or guilt.

D. W. Winnicott offers us a theoretical and developmental account of these ideas about boundaries and self.[1] In his definition of boundaries he actually defines the connection between these two concepts. He says that we can only begin to talk about self-control or internal boundaries when we have a sense of 'I' and 'me' and what he calls 'an integral self', which makes sense of the terms 'inner reality' (me) and 'shared reality' (us, we). The fundamental boundary, Winnicott says, is that which separates the 'me' from the 'not me'. It corresponds to the skin of the body. The fundamental space, he says, is the place within this boundary, inside the body, where the self and inner psychic reality begin to be and grow, to become mature.

Winnicott claims that it is only when we establish a sense of self that we can have an understanding of a boundary differentiating the 'me' and the 'not me'. This means that there is a boundary which encompasses a space, a self, which can fluctuate according to the events, people and interactions the person engages in.

Fritz Perls,[2] the founder of Gestalt psychology, understands this process rather differently. He claims that only when and where the self meets the 'foreign' does the ego come into existence, start to function and determine the boundary between the personal and the impersonal. The boundary, according to Perls, is the point of contact between them. The difference seems to be that Winnicott believes that the self exists and develops and that the baby organizes around it, both according to its own level of development and to the events and people with which it comes into contact. Perls – quite differently – claims that it is only through contact with 'an other' that the ego and the boundaries are defined.

What happens for women?

If we try to examine this issue of boundary and expression of self in relation to women's development, we need to remember Chapter 6, where we talked about the mother–daughter relationship in a patriarchal society. The mother's over-identification with her daughter, her feeling that they are 'the same' and that therefore mother knows what daughter's needs and wants are, makes it difficult for the little girl to have a sense of her own real needs being met by her mother, and to develop a sense of separateness and identity in relation to her mother.

Eichenbaum and Orbach's[3] description in *Outside In, Inside Out* gives an idea of how difficult this issue of self and boundary is for women. 'The experience of initial relating with her mother means that the girl is left with feelings of deprivation, unworthiness and rejection.' Attempts at separation and individuation are frightening. The mother is still vitally important, but may be inhibited in her ability to meet the daughter's real needs. Because of this, the 'needy little girl' part of the daughter's ego has to be split off. It continues to be deprived of the nurturing and contact it needs for maturation. As a consequence, the boundary that should have been constructed between the woman and the outside world, between the 'me' and the 'not me', is constructed internally instead, between herself and her needy, dependent, weak part.

These are, in fact, false boundaries. They come not from an integrated, mature ego structure, but rather from the woman separating one part of herself from another part and keeping the little girl inside shut away from the outside world. This part, then, becomes unacceptable to her, bad, unacknowledged, hidden.

If we try to relate this understanding to her day-to-day experience in the world, what we can see is often a very painful dynamic in her interaction with the outside world. Instead of having a line that will separate 'me' from 'not me', a boundary which implies a selection and negotiation between herself and others, she has a line which separates one part of herself from another. She therefore puts her energy into cutting off that part which she considers as weak, unacceptable, deprived and pained. Actually, this is the part which – if acknowledged and listened to – would indicate her needs, her likes, her wishes and her dislikes.

If we look at this picture in terms of the possible relationships the woman has with people and the world around her, it is as though the border between her and the outside is open – she will therefore be able to know what other people want, but not what she herself wants. She will give to other people what she dares not experience as needing or wanting herself. She will let people and experiences in without any notion of what is good for her, but rather according to what she imagines they would like or want. She takes care of others in the way she would like to have been cared for herself. In short, she says 'no' to a part of herself and more often than not says 'yes' to other people. It is worth saying here that this is in fact what is expected of women in their role as mothers and wives – to know intuitively what the 'other' (baby, husband) wants and needs, and supply it, before considering what they want or need themselves – a 'serving intuition' to make the other grow and mature.

The whole idea of the importance of boundaries has been examined in another strand of feminist psychoanalytic thought. Jean Baker Miller's work in the United States suggests that the essential idea of 'a self' seems to underlie the development of many western notions such as the 'good life', justice, or freedom. But, she contends, the notion of 'a self' does not really fit women's experience. Traditional psychological theory sees all development as a process of separating oneself from others, 'becoming one's own man', achieving an inner sense of separated individuation. She questions the value of these models for both men and women, the real possibility of achieving them in practice and above all their relevance to women's experience. She describes a very different model of development applicable to women, in which both goals and stages of development are defined not by increased progress towards separateness, but, rather, by increased progress towards relatedness.

Baker Miller[4] says that the infant begins to develop a sense of its being as a 'being-in-relationship', a sense of self which reflects what is happening between people. The infant picks up the feelings of the other person. She quotes Surrey:

Surrey has suggested that this early mental representation of the self can be described as a more *encompassing* sense of self by contrast to the more boundaried, more limited, self that is encouraged in boys. She suggests, too, the term 'oscillating' sense of self as compared to the more linear current model, and that 'oscillation' would follow from the ongoing growth of empathy in the child as well as the mother.[5]

Some important implications flow from this radical reformulation. Certain events in later life which are seen as problematic according to other models are seen by Baker Miller as satisfying, motivating and positive. For example, to feel 'more related to another person' does not mean to feel oneself threatened, but to feel oneself enhanced. It does not feel like a loss of part of one's self, but rather a step towards more pleasure and effectiveness. It is the way the girl and woman feel 'things should be'. Being in relationship, picking up the feeling of the other and attending to the 'interaction between' becomes an accepted way of being and acting. It is learned and assumed. It is not alien or threatening. Most important, it is desired.

This way the girl and woman feels a sense of self-worth and self-esteem, based in feeling that she is a part of a relationship and is taking care of the relationship. She often feels a sense of effectiveness as arising out of emotional connections and as bound up with and feeding back into them. This is very different from a sense of effectiveness (or power) based on a sense of lone action and especially from acting against others or over others.

Baker Miller continues to describe childhood and adolescence in this way of perceiving the self not as a static, separate, individual entity, but rather as a part of a relationship, connected, bound up. This is an interesting and positive perspective on a concept that for a long time has been perceived as something negative or problematic in women's psychology.

Boundaries and eating problems

In terms of this concept of boundaries and its relevance to women with eating problems, we can say in very general terms that it relates in two important ways:

(a) Relationship to food and eating.
(b) Body size and body-image.

In relation to food and eating, boundaries may refer to the knowledge of what to eat, when, and how much, coming from inside. For example, knowing when to eat out of stomach hunger rather than according to the clock (a meal every three hours, or three meals a day); how much to eat, not according to diet sheets but, rather, to the point of feeling satisfied; what to eat, according to one's hunger and preferences, not some calorie chart or allowed (usually unpalatable, non-fattening) and forbidden (tasty, fattening, 'naughty') foods. All of these relate to internal control.

In relation to body size and body-image, the woman's body can be seen as a boundary. Women make statements with their bodies. Being a certain body size means something very important in a woman's inner world and her internal as well as external picture or perception of herself. Her body says for her things she is unable to say in actual words; it expresses messages hidden even from herself sometimes.

Women are encouraged from a very early age to be outside themselves, to look at what other people think, need, like, want and appreciate, and to put this before their own needs and opinions. A woman is encouraged, in other words, to use her centre for attending to other people's growth and for the development of *their* centres. Her self becomes secondary in importance, in immediacy, in respect. She is not encouraged to develop a self and identity of her own. She is a mother, a housewife, a daughter – identities that on the one hand, by their nature and aim, are centred in the other, and on the other hand are devalued and thought of as non-identity.

In terms of boundaries and expression of the self, we can say in simple terms that the anorexic has her boundaries very tightly held, not letting a lot come in or go out. She doesn't need people, she claims by her behaviour, not relationships, care or love, not even the most essential element of our living – food. She says 'no' to almost everything. The compulsive eater says 'yes' to almost everything. The bulimic says 'yes', but then a very violent 'no'.

The anorexic's self is completely invested in self-denial. In her refusal of the outside world, she creates a person in her head who has no needs at all, who is above needs. Her boundaries, therefore, have to be very tight; without thinking of her own needs and wishes she says an automatic 'no'. The compulsive eater says 'yes' to food, people, whatever comes her way – without, again, considering her own wishes, likes, dislikes or needs. In her mind she is trying to please others, to give them what they need, or what she believes they do. She has needs which she feels ashamed and frightened of and which she tries to cut off. One way she does this is through eating, to push these needs away, another through projecting them on to others and trying to fulfil them for others. Her boundaries are very open and her self is invested in meeting others' needs and pleasing them. She gives to others what she would like to have received herself. She does for them what she wishes had been done for her.

For the bulimic woman, again, the issue of boundaries and expression of self is double-edged. Because of her desperate need that her façade should be 'good' and acceptable to others, because it is her image, that part she presents to the world as her good self, her boundaries have to be quite open. She lets people, food, care, relationships in quite easily, in order to be acceptable, likeable, a 'good girl'. However, because she has a hidden part that is 'bad' and secretive and must not be discovered, everything that comes in is allowed up to that point where the hidden part is not seen, and then, when the 'danger' of being found out is felt, it all needs to be thrown out again, like the food – vomited out. Her sense of her self is invested in the 'good girl' image, and in rejecting anything or anybody that tries to pass that boundary into the forbidden, terrible part of herself which is unacceptable to her and, she assumes, will be to others. A good example may be if someone pays her a compliment: she hears it, says 'thank you', and immediately doubts begin to arise – 'If only they knew my real, hidden part (what I am really like inside) they would not think good things about me' – so the compliment loses its value for her.

Boundaries in therapy

What we have just described as the compulsive eater's, the anorexic's and the bulimic's relationship with people around them and the world outside applies in a similar way to the therapeutic relationship. We shall describe it in much more detail later, in the chapters about our therapeutic approach; here we just want to mention briefly the ways in which these concepts and issues are relevant to therapy.

The issue of boundaries is crucially important, both in the

Boundary and Self

content and context of therapy. The woman comes to the therapeutic relationship bringing her distress, her need and desire to be helped, her wish for her problems to disappear (mostly she wants the therapist to take them away, to cure her, to 'do it' for her magically). She also brings her anxieties, her fears, her pain, anger and disappointment.

In the beginning stages it is extremely important that the therapy is experienced as a safe place for the client to be able to express her dependence, her vulnerability, her feelings. Her defence will be her internal boundaries – in other words, she will be protecting the little girl inside, hidden away from the therapist, as she is used to doing. This part of herself is usually cut off. She feels it is dangerous and unlovable. She is sure that this part of herself will be rejected by the therapist, as will her needs. Her existence and her capacity to be loved and valued – she believes – are based on not exposing that needy, dependent part of her. Her sense of self is poor; she does not know what she wants, likes or needs; she feels empty. If she cannot experience or talk about that part of herself, she needs to be encouraged to express her fears and anxieties about what would happen if she did.

Clear boundaries on the part of the therapist are therefore very important and contribute to that sense of safety. The sessions should last for a certain length of time, at a regular time. The therapist must always be there on time, to create continuity. The space should be the same for all sessions, there should be a clear contract, and the therapist must know how and when to say 'yes' and 'no' appropriately, according to her professional ethical codes as well as her feelings and knowledge. All separations, long or short, must be dealt with in the sessions (holidays as well as the meaning of missed sessions). The therapist should have a clear boundary which keeps her own personal life and her problems outside her relationship with her client.

These contextual boundaries give room for the woman – symbolically – to open her internal boundaries and let the little girl inside be expressed: her dependence needs, her wish to be cared for, her anger about the therapist not being there for her on demand, and so on. Eventually she may begin to feel and experience herself as more of a whole person, expressing more of the parts she never dared even to acknowledge existed. Nurturing and care in the relationship may replace food, which was previously considered the only constant, timeless, spaceless presence for her.

Fighting Food

The woman's understanding of herself will bring her a better knowledge of her needs as well as of her boundaries.

Boundaries within families

We first learn about our boundaries and develop a sense of ourselves within our families. In a real sense, our ability to know who we are both in relation to other people and distinct from them depends on our parents having this knowledge and feelings about themselves. Each family has its own particular norms and unspoken rules about its boundaries. The boundary which surrounds some families is very tight and closed. Such families do not easily let 'outsiders' in, and can make it hard for family members to leave. In other families, there is an 'open house'. Friends and neighbours are welcome and there is no very rigid distinction between family members, members of the extended family and others. Cultural patterns, including social class and racial differences, are important here. Much of our understanding about boundaries is transmitted through culture.

Within the family itself, there is great variation in how separate people are and feel in relation to each other. In some families, individuality and privacy are very highly prized and it can sometimes be difficult for individuals to feel close, to share, to really have a sense of relatedness to each other. On the other hand, there are families where a need for privacy is experienced as a rejection. Everything should be shared, everyone has to know everything about everyone else. In these families, even feelings are family property. It can be impossible for one person to be upset without affecting the whole family.

In the families of women who go on to develop eating disorders, we often find that there are or have been difficulties with boundaries. We have already discussed the ways in which mothers and daughters can end up with boundaries which are very blurred. Separation between mother and daughter is a difficult process and often is never fully achieved. A woman who has never really achieved a sense of separateness from her own mother may well choose a partner who to some extent satisfies her need to be merged with another person. They in turn will have children who they expect to be an extension of their own merged relationship. Growing up in such a family can present a child, especially a girl, with great difficulties in defining her own boundaries and developing a sense of self. Any attempt at separation can, in some families, be interpreted as rejection; any assertion of a personal preference or opinion can be taken as a criticism of the family.

It has been pointed out by several authors that there appears to be a link between sexual abuse in childhood and the later development of eating disorders.[6] Whenever sexual abuse occurs within a family, it points to a lack of boundaries, to an inability of the family to acknowledge that a child's body is her own. We have worked with a number of women who have been victims of sexual abuse, sometimes within the family, more often from adults outside the family, and what these women tend to have in common is an inability to assert their rights over their own bodies – in fact, no belief that they had any right to draw their own boundaries and say 'no' to adults. These extreme cases of lack of boundaries leading to sexual abuse can perhaps be seen as part of a continuum. Families who believe that they know what their children want to eat and attempt to force their own preferences upon them regardless of the child's own wants and needs are similarly denying the child's autonomy and her rights to take in what she wants. Many of the women who come asking for help with their eating problems initially describe their families as 'close' and 'loving'. Some time later it may emerge that relationships have actually been so close that it has been difficult for the developing girl to experience herself as an autonomous individual with her own particular needs and rights which could be safely asserted without offence or a sense of rejection towards others.

NOTES

1 M. Davis and D. Wallbridge (1981): *Boundary and Space: An Introduction to the Work of D.W. Winnicott*, Penguin, Harmondsworth.

2 F. S. Perls (1969): *Ego Hunger and Aggression*, Vintage, New York.

3 L. Eichenbaum and S. Orbach (1982): *Outside In, Inside Out*, Penguin, Harmondsworth.

4 J. Baker Miller (1984): 'The Development of a Woman's Sense of Self', unpublished paper from the Stone Centre, Wellesley College, Mass.

5 Surrey, J. (1984): 'The Self in Relation: A Theory of Women's

Development', *Work in Progress*, 84–02, Stone Centre, Wellesley College, working papers series.

6 R. Oppenheimer, K. Howells, R. L. Palmer and D. A. Chaloner (1985): 'Adverse sexual experiences in childhood and clinical eating disorders: a preliminary description', *Journal of Psychiatric Research*, 19, 357–61.

8
MISCONCEPTIONS AND COMMON APPROACHES TO TREATMENT

In this chapter, we shall begin by looking at some of the ways in which eating disorders are commonly misunderstood. We shall go on to show that these misunderstandings of the problems involved can lead to treatments which are not only ineffective, but which can be positively damaging.

According to the point of view we have been arguing so far, the fundamental misconception about eating disorders which permeates most of the professional literature is that eating disorders are really about eating. This misconception underlies most of the major treatment initiatives which have been developed over the last century. In order to understand eating disorders properly, we need to begin by seeing the symptoms as a metaphor for or symbolic representation of another kind of reality. It is not that the symptoms themselves are irrelevant; on the contrary, it is the symptoms, the patterns of disordered eating, which point us towards an understanding of what it is that the woman is seeking to communicate. Far from ignoring symptoms, we need to look at them carefully and attempt to translate them into the reality of the woman's inner world. The problem with traditional approaches to eating disorders is their tendency to treat the symptoms as though they really are the problem in themselves. Thus the aim in compulsive eating is seen simply as stopping the woman from eating so much. In anorexia, many professionals behave as if by restoring weight they will really solve the anorexic's problem. Bulimia, it is commonly thought, can be solved simply by regulating the woman's eating pattern without giving any attention to the underlying problems which her eating expresses.

Compulsive eating – the diet 'solution'
As we have already seen, most compulsive eaters are also compulsive dieters. While a woman may have several episodes of overeating during the week, she will probably also have two or

three days on which she eats very little, begins the 'new diet' and tries to compensate for having overeaten. Health professionals and advisers are generally concerned only with dealing with the effects of compulsive eating. Obesity is generally recognized as a problem, whereas compulsive eating itself is not. The compulsive eater is therefore normally offered help with her problem only if she becomes seriously overweight. The help she is most likely to be offered? A diet. By definition, the compulsive eater feels out of control around food. She is out of touch with sensations of physical hunger; she uses food to meet needs unconnected with physical hunger. In addition to this, she may have spent many years trying to control her food intake, without success. It is therefore very unlikely that a new diet will be effective simply because it has been suggested by a doctor or dietician.

Women eat compulsively because they feel in some sense deprived, emotionally. A diet can only increase that sense of deprivation and eventually the woman will rebel and break her diet. We also know that some women who eat compulsively have an unconscious wish and need to be fat. Until this wish can be explored, made conscious and resolved, the woman will continue to sabotage her own conscious attempts to lose weight.

It is an unfortunate fact that the cycle of dieting followed by 'breaking out' of the diet and overeating is a pattern which is actually likely to increase weight. When the body is deprived of food, as in a diet, the metabolism tends to slow down, to conserve what nourishment is available. When the diet stops and is followed by overeating, this additional unexpected food is not burned up at the same rate as it would have been if the food intake had been moderate and continuous. This leads to the regaining of a lot of weight in a short time, further confirming to the woman how dangerous food is to her.

Some commercial organizations offer 'support' to women who are attempting to diet. This support invariably amounts to weighing and checking up on women, encouraging them to 'confess' when they have allowed themselves something they wanted which is forbidden, and sometimes even humiliating women if they gain weight. The only support this kind of approach really offers is support for women's feelings that they really are worthless, greedy and out of control. Although a woman may manage for a while to be a 'good girl', she will never succeed in learning what it is her body wants and needs, or what her other needs are which are not connected with food. These approaches, which focus on women's weight and attempt to enforce a loss, very rarely produce any lasting benefit either in terms of slimming or in the way women feel about themselves.

We must also remember that the diet business has become big business. To invent and market a new diet is probably one of the quickest ways to become a millionaire.

So when the diets fail – what next?

Drugs

Twenty years or so ago, it was quite common for women to be prescribed amphetamines as 'slimming pills'. Amphetamines, or 'uppers' as they are sometimes known, are powerful addictive drugs which produce restlessness, overactivity and an illusion of well-being. They also suppress the appetite. They can cause psychotic reactions, heart failure and coma. They invariably produce insomnia, which leads to the use of tranquillizing drugs or 'downers' to induce sleep.

While most doctors nowadays believe that amphetamines are too dangerous to prescribe for weight reduction, we have certainly met women whose doctors do prescribe them. Other, more modern drugs, such as femfluramine, commonly prescribed for obesity, while not having some of the most dangerous effects of amphetamines, still produce restlessness, sleeplessness and a false sense of well-being, invariably followed by depression. These kinds of drugs have a particularly damaging psychological effect. They enable women whose underlying problem is a neediness which cannot be expressed to believe falsely that they can manage on less and less while doing more and more. Effectively, they encourage women to suppress and cover up the needy, non-coping part of themselves still more.

Surgery and other medical procedures

It seems that as long as our society continues to loathe fatness and to regard obesity as a disability, the medical profession will devise more and more bizarre means for attempting to make women thin – and some women at least will be desperate enough to try them.

Fighting Food

We have often heard women who eat compulsively say that they wish they could simply be stopped from eating – that they could just be prevented from ingesting food. Not surprisingly, doctors have come up with an answer. Jaw wiring.

It seems incredible that any woman would willingly subject herself to this humiliating and cruel procedure, and indeed we do not know how many have, but jaw wiring has certainly been put forward as the only means of controlling the compulsive eater. It is a procedure which involves a temporary closing of the jaw by wiring the teeth together so that only liquid foods can be taken. The fact that the woman cannot speak properly, cannot kiss and for that matter cannot even clean her teeth seems a small price to pay. Of course, such enforced starvation leads to weight loss, but at what cost? And clearly, as soon as the wires are removed and the woman begins to eat compulsively again, she will gain weight.

For some years, surgeons have been called upon to provide the answer to compulsive eating. A number of different operations have been designed to cut and seal the stomach and gastric tract so that food taken passes more or less directly out again without being absorbed as nourishment. This procedure is generally known as 'gastric bypass'. The latest development appears to be the Jejunojejunostomy.[1] This operation involves a stapling of the stomach as well as a gastric bypass. According to the authors of the paper describing the procedure, 'gastric bypass is our procedure of choice for treatment of morbid obesity', although they admit that 'the cause of obesity is unclear'. Whatever the result of such dramatic interventions in terms of weight loss, none of the women concerned have any chance of learning the difference between hunger stimulated by their stomachs and the emotional hunger they feel. There are also some dubious physical consequences of such operations. 'A massive weight loss will often leave the patient with large amounts of redundant skin that pose cosmetic and hygienic problems ... Reduction of abdominal skin aprons, breast reduction, and upper arm and thigh contouring are some of the most commonly required procedures.' Several plastic surgery operations will be needed to make her 'acceptable'. Out of a series of 100 such operations, the authors report 'complications' in twenty-five. These complications range from wound infection and incidental splenectomy to pulmonary embolus, deep vein thrombosis, ulcer and hernia. We can only ask why it is that women will go to such appalling and life-threatening lengths to be thin. And why it is that no one is prepared to try to find out.

Anorexia nervosa

In 1874 William Gull, the English physician who gave anorexia nervosa its name, advised the following plan of treatment: 'The patients should be fed at regular intervals, and surrounded by persons who could have moral control over them, relations and friends being generally the worst attendants.'

Gull had neither the expertise nor the necessary conceptual framework for understanding anorexia as a symptom expressing an underlying psychological conflict. It is therefore not surprising that he should focus exclusively on correcting the most obvious symptom of anorexia, the weight loss. What should surprise us, though, is that with the passing of more than a century and with all the advances in our knowledge and understanding, anorexia is still often treated in very much the same way that Gull suggested. Most contemporary writers on anorexia acknowledge that weight loss is merely a symptom. Many also insist that psychotherapy is vital to any resolution of the underlying problems. In spite of these encouraging developments, the actual experience of most women treated for anorexia is that the focus is almost exclusively on the physical effects of the disorder.

It has to be said that there is no uniform treatment for anorexia in the UK or in the United States. Medical opinions about treatment vary, and there is a vast difference in the availability and quality of facilities across the country. In metropolitan centres there are often specialist wards or units with experienced staff and a clear policy for treating anorexia. In rural areas, anorexics are likely to be treated by staff with little experience and may often find themselves admitted to general psychiatric wards and treated alongside confused elderly people and very disturbed people with serious mental illnesses. There is not even a general policy of anorexia being treated as a psychiatric disorder at all. In many parts of the country the young anorexic will be referred to a physician, and if hospitalized she will find herself among patients with a variety of physical illnesses.

The issue of weight gain

Anorexia nervosa is a disorder which can undoubtedly have very serious physical consequences. While any effective treatment needs to focus on the underlying conflicts and difficulties, the therapist can never afford to disregard the severity of the symptoms. However, many traditional approaches to treatment focus almost exclusively on the physical effects of anorexia, paying little attention to what the symptoms actually mean and what is causing them.

This concentration on the physical consequences of the disorder has led to a policy of routine hospitalization for anorexia, in order to achieve an increase in weight. In most hospitals a 'target weight' is set, which is usually the average weight for the woman's height. In theory, she will not be allowed to leave until this weight is achieved. In practice, however, many women discharge themselves before they reach this target weight and as the process is usually so lengthy and difficult, doctors commonly give up and agree to discharge at a lower weight.

Procedures for increasing weight vary from one hospital to another. 'Treatment' always consists of large amounts of food high in calories – often as much as 4,000 calories a day. There are a number of techniques used for ensuring that this food is consumed. Sometimes the 'patient' will simply be cajoled, persuaded and nagged into eating. She will be kept in bed, not allowed to go to the bathroom and watched constantly in case she should try to dispose of the food by hiding it or vomiting it up. Under certain treatment regimes, she will be given tranquillizing medication in order to make her less resistant to eating and gaining weight.

Certain hospitals have adopted and still practise a regime of 'behaviour modification', even though this was criticized and largely discredited by Hilde Bruch as long ago as 1974.[2] The object of this form of treatment is to reward the woman when she eats and to punish her when she does not. In its most extreme form, behaviour modification involves taking away from her everything which makes life comfortable and even bearable. She may have no radio, no books, no visitors – perhaps not even a pillow. She can earn these 'privileges' only as she gains weight.

Not surprisingly, such 'treatment' sometimes works in terms of a rapid increase in weight. But what are its real effects? As we have already described, the woman in an anorexic phase feels terrified of putting on weight. She feels an intense need to be in control of her body and of everything she puts into it. To her, maintaining such control feels like a matter of life and death. If a woman in an anorexic phase is admitted to hospital, she usually has the experience of all her control being taken away from her. While we, on the outside, can see that her obsession with controlling her weight and her body simply masks and conceals her lack of control in any other areas of her life, she herself is not aware of this and can feel only her desperate need to stay thin.

Anorexia is a defence, a defence against feeling needy, dependent and bad. This is what she is trying to control. To take away her control in such a brutal and humiliating way makes her feel a total and awful failure, as though she has lost everything. All too often, the anorexic woman will quite literally eat herself out of hospital, only to begin trying to restore her self-esteem by once again losing weight when she is discharged. According to Bruch, a rigid, punitive re-feeding regime which does not pay attention to the underlying disorder can lead to profound depression and even suicide.

From our experience, we can also say very clearly that such an approach simply does not work. Year after year, we have seen hundreds of women who have subjected themselves to hospital treatment for anorexia only to be discharged in despair and with none of the real problems addressed. It is, of course, the nature of the re-feeding treatment offered which makes so many anorexics determined to avoid it, and which can lead young women who really want help to deny that they have a problem for months or even years. When women in an anorexic phase understandably resist attempts to increase their weight and express their sense of powerlessness by trying to hide food or talking nurses into 'letting them off', they are often called deceitful or manipulative. Not only are these labels unhelpful, but if we consider just what it is that the anorexic is being subjected to we may find her behaviour more understandable.

Anorexia itself serves as an expression of selfhood. By her refusal to eat, she says: 'This is me.' She therefore experiences re-feeding as an annihilation of her sense of self, which throws her back to times in her childhood when she also felt her self annihilated.

While we can clearly see the damaging effects of such

unsympathetic experiences of hospitalization which take away the anorexic woman's control, we should perhaps ask the more fundamental question – is hospitalization always or even often necessary? Is it necessary for the anorexic woman to put on weight before she can benefit from therapeutic help which addresses the true underlying source of her distress? Some specialists believe that weight gain is a necessary prerequisite to psychotherapy, that women at a low weight cannot embark on therapy. We have found, however, that women whose weight is low but stable can certainly benefit from therapy, and that given the right kind of help they will, in their own time, gain weight. We would go further and suggest that far from enforced weight gain making a woman more receptive to therapy, it very often has the opposite effect. A woman who has been forced and sometimes tricked into putting on weight will end up with feelings of betrayal. She may well feel that her only hope is to try to put her life together on her own as best she can, without accepting any help from anyone. At the very least, before she can benefit from any therapeutic help she will have to work through all her feelings about the painful experience of hospitalization.

Annette was eighteen when she had her first anorexic episode and twenty-three by the time she came in to therapy. She lost weight dramatically while studying for her A-levels and was admitted to the local psychiatric hospital, where her weight was increased from $6\frac{1}{2}$ stone to nearly 8. Following her discharge, she was profoundly depressed and unable to resume her school work. Even worse, from Annette's point of view, her eating went quite out of control. She began to take large quantities of laxatives and to vomit after eating in order to try to prevent herself gaining any more weight. In spite of the hospital admission, Annette's problems had not in any way diminished and neither had her preoccupation with her weight.

Things came to a head in June when she took an overdose of her mother's sleeping tablets. She was admitted to hospital and this time it was recognized that Annette had problems apart from her weight. It was felt, perhaps quite rightly, that many of Annette's difficulties lay within her family. Family therapy was judged the right course of action, but unfortunately this option was not adequately discussed with Annette and her family. After the first session, the family felt too upset to continue and once again

Annette was left to deal with her difficulties alone. She began a rigid restricting diet and a regime of punishing exercise, and by Christmas she once again weighed 6½ stone. She was just nineteen. Things at home had become so bad, with Annette's constant refusal of food and her parents' desperation, that the family doctor arranged another admission to hospital, this time a large city psychiatric hospital with considerable experience of treating anorexia. Here Annette faced a regime as rigid as the self-punishing one she had constructed for herself, but this time the aim was for her to gain weight rather than lose it. She was given a single room, with no television, no radio and no books. She was not allowed visitors. Her target weight of 9 stone was set without consultation, and a hierarchy of 'privileges' was drawn up which she could 'earn' by gaining weight. She had little option but to comply, but by the time she reached 7½ stone she was so distraught that her parents took her home.

Annette was depressed but self-contained. She immediately reduced her weight to just below 7 stone and vowed never to see a doctor again. Although very withdrawn and quite unable to make friends or sustain relationships, she took A-levels at a local college and gained a place at a polytechnic. She was still completely preoccupied with her body and her weight. During her first year, her eating again became chaotic, she was still unable to make friends and she felt that she was on the edge of a breakdown. She was finally persuaded by a fellow student to go to the college counselling service, and from here she was finally referred for psychotherapy. It had taken six years from the time she first became ill for anyone to attempt to offer Annette any help which went beyond her symptoms. Regrettably, Annette's story is typical of many we have heard.

Bulimia

Until quite recently, there was no specific treatment for women who express their distress by constantly overeating and then making themselves sick, or taking vast numbers of laxatives to purge themselves of food. Many bulimic women do not ask for treatment. The symptom is a secret one, and women feel too ashamed to let anyone know about it. In recent years, when there have been some sympathetic portrayals of the problem in books and in the media, women have begun to ask for help.

We have heard many reports from women of being met with horror and disbelief by their family doctors. The most common advice given to women is simply to stop doing it! Doctors would not dream of giving such naïve advice to drug addicts or alcoholics. In spite of the fact that in a simple sense it is their behaviour which causes their difficulties, it is universally acknowledged that without help, they will not be able to break their self-destructive cycle.

One of the difficulties that bulimic women have in getting their problem taken seriously is that on the surface most are competent, successful women. They give the impression of being able to cope well with life and so tend to elicit a telling-off for their stupid behaviour, rather than an offer of help.

When bulimia was first recognized as a clinical entity separate from both anorexia and compulsive eating, there was nonetheless a tendency to admit bulimic women to hospital and treat them very much like anorexics. It was thought that what the bulimic woman needed to do was to regulate her eating pattern, to learn how to eat 'normally'. Bulimic women were 'prescribed' the correct amount of food – no more, no less – and this, it was expected, would bestow upon the woman the ability to control her intake of food.

This kind of approach, though on the face of it quite sensible, ignores the fact that the bulimia expresses the hidden, largely unconscious aspect of the woman's personality which feels totally out of control. We have noted with great concern that a number of women who have given up expressing the messy, confused, muddled part of themselves through food have adopted an even more self-destructive means of dealing with it, such as abusing alcohol or drugs.

Overcoming the dangerous symptom of bulimia cannot truly be achieved by simply changing the unwanted piece of behaviour. The underlying difficulty, if not made conscious, understood and worked through, will simply reassert itself elsewhere. Maureen was one such young woman. She had become preoccupied with controlling her weight when she was in her late teens, and although she kept her weight at an artificially low level it never dropped low enough to alarm anyone or to produce the diagnosis of anorexia. On the surface, her life went well. She left school and gained a place on a prestigious vocational course in hotel management. She was an attractive young woman with a warm and bubbly personality, yet underneath this was a frightened, insecure person and Maureen often had the feeling of not being real at all.

In an increasingly competitive situation, Maureen set even more store by her appearance. She was terribly afraid of becoming overweight and began to vomit after meals to control her weight. She quickly began to use her vomiting to relieve her anxiety and to distract her from the loneliness she felt. Maureen had the ability to make friends but always felt she had to show the happy, cheerful, carefree part of herself, which felt increasingly unreal. Feeling more and more depressed, Maureen knew that something was badly wrong. She asked for help with her eating problem and was referred for a six-week 'programme' at the day centre of a local psychiatric hospital. Here she was told of the dangers of self-induced vomiting and given kindly advice about her diet. She was asked to keep a diary of her food intake and each morning she was given the opportunity to talk about how it was going. Maureen tried hard not to vomit and did succeed in greatly reducing the incidence of her vomiting. At the day centre, she joined an on-going group, but everyone's problems seemed so much more serious than her own that Maureen was unable to disclose how depressed she felt. Instead, she appeared pleasant and was helpful and popular with the other patients. When her time was up, Maureen left the centre and returned to her course. She was told she could go back whenever she wanted.

She continued to struggle with her wish to vomit, but found instead that she was drinking a lot and that this temporarily relieved her depression. She was going out less and less and losing contact with her friends. She was persuaded to go to a college party, where she met a young man, and her loneliness propelled her into an intense sexual relationship, which was shortlived. Feeling even more depressed and in despair with herself, Maureen had several other such relationships. She was drinking more and more and still her real feelings were kept a secret. On the face of it, she seemed to be 'having fun'. But Maureen hated the life-style she had drifted into. It did not satisfy her and left her real distress and unhappiness untouched. Gradually, she withdrew from people, back to her old way of dealing with her problems – food.

What Maureen, like other bulimic women, needed was the

opportunity really to encounter and explore the feelings which her bulimia obscured. Far from learning to cover up or to 'regulate' the feelings which seemed so out of control and terrifying, it is precisely these feelings which need to be brought into consciousness and integrated so that it becomes possible and more comfortable to live with the whole self.

We have seen that many of the common responses to eating disorders are ineffective and that some are positively damaging. The reasons for the alarming failure to make progress in the treatment of eating disorders lies in the inability of many professionals to understand their symbolic nature. Eating disorders are best understood as metaphors of a woman's inner reality. To try to treat simply the disordered eating behaviour itself is to become enmeshed in the metaphor and to fail to grasp its meaning.

A final problem associated with many of the current treatment initiatives for all eating disorders is their impatience. Eating disorders point to serious difficulties; they are not simple little symptoms which can easily be 'cleared up'.

We acknowledge that resources for treating eating disorders are pitifully inadequate and that many practitioners have to provide a service within impossible financial constraints. Nonetheless, we feel it very important to make clear that treatment and recovery do take time. To offer a woman who has perhaps had a series of eating problems and other related symptoms over a number of years a treatment programme lasting only a few weeks is not to invite success. The woman may gain something from it, but unless it is made clear to her that further help will be needed and is available, she may take away from the whole experience a sense of failure and hopelessness.

It is of course questionable whether resources are wisely used at present. In-patient treatment for anorexia is very expensive, as is surgery for compulsive eating. Out-patient psychotherapy is very much cheaper, even if it is long-term. Self-help initiatives supported by professionals are one of the least costly forms of treatment and are often preferred by sufferers themselves.

In summary, it seems clear that at the moment many treatment approaches are not driven by consumer choice, by negotiation with women about what they want and what might help. The more rational and humane treatment of many groups of problems can be hampered and constrained by tradition and convention. Eating disorders are no exception.

NOTES

1 F. E. Rosato and M. Matthews, 'Surgical Treatment in Morbid Obesity', in H. L. Field and B. B. Domangue (eds.) (1987): *Eating Disorders Throughout the Life Span*, Praeger, New York.

2 H. Bruch (1974): *Eating Disorders*, Routledge & Kegan Paul, London.

9
DEVELOPING A PSYCHOTHERAPEUTIC APPROACH

Eating disorders and psychotherapy

Throughout the book so far, we have been concerned to communicate a particular way of understanding eating disorders. It is an understanding born out of our own experience and has evolved and changed over many years. It is not, however, our intention merely to aid understanding. Although it is vital to understand the complex social and psychological themes which contribute to eating disorders, it is also essential that this understanding leads on to a clear and thoughtful response on the part of those wishing to work with such problems. In writing this section of the book, we hope that we will have something to say which will be of value to therapists and counsellors working in the field, as well as to general practitioners, teachers and other professional groups who are concerned in the process of referral and who may need guidance about what kind of help it is best to encourage women to seek. We are also concerned to try to explain and communicate something about a psychotherapeutic approach to the women who suffer from eating disorders. Deciding to look for help is a difficult enough decision in itself; considering what kind of help to seek can be fraught with problems for those who may be feeling particularly anxious and vulnerable. We hope that this chapter will point to a direction, while the section on Finding Help (pp. 171–4) will offer some concrete suggestions.

Psychotherapy is a discipline, deriving largely from psychoanalysis, which seeks to make sense of human distress in terms of the internal world of the individual. This internal world is built up from all the experiences, present and past, of the individual and, perhaps more importantly, how the individual herself has perceived, taken in and interpreted these experiences.

The tool of psychotherapy is the therapeutic relationship and it is through and within this relationship that growth and change can occur. It is a joint undertaking, something which requires patience and dedication on behalf of therapist and client and is used successfully to treat a variety of psychological difficulties. In the UK, where psychotherapy is probably not as readily available and acceptable as it is in some other countries, it is not a form of treatment which is readily prescribed for eating disorders. The majority of the women we have worked with have been offered a variety of the physical treatments before finding their way to a therapist.

Why is there such reluctance to offer psychotherapy to women with eating disorders? In the previous chapter, we reviewed some of the treatments currently available and saw that most of these respond directly to the symptom of disordered eating. From our perspective, to engage with the woman at the level of her eating behaviour is to make the same kind of mistake which the woman herself is making. It is to concentrate on the symptom, rather than on the underlying problems and feelings which produce it. It is to mistake the metaphor, the coded statement, for the reality which underlies it. Having said that, it is an understandable mistake. Eating disorders are so dramatic in their presentation that it can feel hard to resist intervening at the level of the physical symptom. Later we shall discuss how the psychotherapist might go about maintaining just such a resistance. So part of the problem in formulating a helpful therapeutic response lies in the very nature of the symptoms, and also sometimes in the entreaties of the women themselves, who more than anything plead with us to help rid them of these symptoms. But there is something more. By the very nature of the problems which underlie eating disorders, these problems can at a first glance seem very difficult to treat with psychotherapy.

The feature which all eating disorders have in common is that they represent, symbolically, the difficulties which women have in taking in anything for themselves. These difficulties are displayed via food; the reality is emotional. The woman with an eating disorder is showing us how difficult she finds it to identify, express and meet her own needs for care, concern and nurturance. Given this basic difficulty, women with eating disorders do initially find it difficult to respond to psychotherapy. If you are unable to recognize and acknowledge what it is you need, what your real feelings are and what help you need, it will be an enormous problem to use what a psychotherapist has to offer and to find ways of using her help. This may mean that professionals, sensing that making a therapeutic approach will be difficult, suggest something else instead, not understanding that this resistance has to be overcome and worked through before change can occur. The really vital point is that given the difficulties the woman has in taking things in, the only way she is likely to resolve her problems is through a therapeutic relationship.

The idea of therapy as feeding

All women with eating disorders have quite specific difficulties in making and sustaining relationships. These may be very apparent, as with the anorexic who clearly rejects contact with other people, or it may be less obvious. The compulsive eater may have many friends and acquaintances, indeed she may be constantly preoccupied with other people's lives and problems. But although she cannot say no to anyone, no one really gets close to her, no one can really help her to meet her needs. She uses people compulsively, in the way she uses food, but never feels satisfied by either. The bulimic woman can often make relationships and can temporarily feel valued, but beneath this she feels alone and rejected, sure that no one really cares for her or can help her. She vomits up care and concern from other people in the same way that she gets rid of her food. It can never stay with her, can never really nourish her.

All these patterns will become evident in the therapy, and it is within a therapeutic relationship that the problems can be made conscious, acknowledged and worked through. In many respects, psychotherapy echoes and resembles the relationship with the mother or carer in the earliest stages of life. The therapist endeavours to focus full attention on the client, following, understanding and commenting upon all of her feelings, reactions and changes of mood. This is exactly what the 'good enough' mother or carer does with the tiny baby, particularly when she feeds it. The crucial difference, of course, is that the mother does her best to meet the real needs of the baby, while the therapist, though able to meet the need for understanding, can sometimes only comment upon other real-life needs which she is unable to meet. Although the therapist does not literally feed the client as the mother does the baby, symbolically this is just what she does. As well as paying very careful attention, the therapist uses her own intuitive feeling responses to help her understand the client's situation. This process of being understood can be in itself a healing experience and can be accompanied by enormous relief. On the other hand, it creates immense feelings of dependence and stirs up a profound well of feelings related to needs which were and remain unmet. For women with eating disorders who have such problems with their dependent needy feelings, this is not a comfortable experience; on the contrary, it can feel terrifying. The woman can feel exposed, with no defences, and, above all, full of the confusing needs which she has striven so hard to banish from her consciousness. This can make her want to turn away from the therapist and all that she has to offer. She finds the therapist's nourishment, her symbolic food, no easier to handle than food itself. And yet if she is to have a chance to resolve her difficulties with her life and with her food, it is vital that she engage in a process in which all her feelings can be explored and worked through with another person. The very issues which will make psychotherapy a difficult process for the woman with an eating disorder also make it an essential one. Much as she might resist it, resent it and try to deny it, the woman with an eating disorder desperately needs food; good, nourishing food in manageable quantities, which will remain constant however she might change.

Starting therapy

For a woman with an eating disorder, asking for help represents perhaps one of the most difficult decisions she will ever make. She wants and needs help desperately, but at the same time fears and dreads having to acknowledge her own neediness and to rely on another person. She knows that she will have to confront the part of herself which all her symptoms with food have helped her to obscure for so long. Overcoming her resistance to seeking help in itself amounts to an enormous shift in attitude, and it is very important for the therapist to be aware of this and of what it means for the client. She may have sought help before, and her experience of doing so may well have been an unhappy one. Many professionals do have a rather negative and hostile attitude to eating disorders, and it is important to examine these feelings so that the would-be therapist can be more in touch with her own feelings and in a position to develop a more compassionate stance.

The feelings of the therapist

The compulsive eater is stereotyped as a person who is weak, greedy and lacking in self-control. As with clients with other sorts of compulsions, there is a danger that the therapist will feel critical, dismissive and wish to control her. Anorexic women, on the other hand, often inspire feelings of fear, awe and envy in therapists. The control which the anorexic woman seems to exert over both her body and her feelings can make her seem very distant and difficult to reach. Many therapists are reluctant to take anorexic women on for therapy, as the anorexic stance can seem so intimidating. Bulimia is a symptom which brings out feelings of contempt in many people. Apart from seeming physically disgusting and repellent, the waste involved can make it feel almost self-indulgent. If the therapist communicates any of these feelings to a bulimic client, she will simply be confirming what the woman already feels about herself. In many years of running courses and training sessions for therapists working with women with eating disorders, we have found an enormous range of very personal reactions and associations with this particular group of clients. These personal responses are no bar to working with such women; indeed, everyone is bound to have an emotional reaction to such dramatic symptoms. The important issue is for therapists to understand their personal feelings and to know that they *are* personal feelings, which are quite different from therapeutic responses. For example, if a first meeting with an anorexic client leaves the therapist feeling big, clumsy, awkward and very much in awe of the fragile, contained little being in the consulting room (and this is a common reaction), the therapist needs to become fully aware of these feelings and to understand that the client is defending herself against her own sense of being too big, messy and without boundaries. The therapist is thus able to empathize with the woman's underlying dilemma, without simply reacting to the projection of these anxieties on to her.

Managing the symptoms

The very dramatic symptoms which eating disorders can present very often and understandably create a great deal of anxiety in therapists. Anorexia, perhaps more than any other psychological disorder, appears very frightening and can indeed be dangerous. Bulimia too, particularly if it involves the abuse of laxatives as well as vomiting, can lead to serious physical consequences and even death. In the short term, compulsive eating does not normally carry such dire risks but the symptom and the distress it produces in the client can make the therapist feel very frustrated. If the client is very obese, which can be dangerous, she can feel a great responsibility for the client's weight, particularly if this continues to increase, and a sense of impotence to help the client with it. With all eating disorders, although the therapist needs to be aware of the meanings of the symptoms and alert to their possible seriousness, it is nonetheless important that they are not allowed to dominate the therapy situation with the frustration and anxiety they can produce. We shall look at each in turn and discuss ways in which the therapist might go about managing the symptoms.

Anorexia

While weight is obviously a crucial issue when beginning therapy with an anorexic woman, the therapeutic aim is to deal with it compassionately and safely so that it does not become the dominant issue. While some writers believe that low weight is in itself an obstacle to therapy, we have had considerable success in treating anorexics with a low but stable weight. It is always unrealistic to expect a woman in an acute anorexic phase to increase her weight before she can be offered any help. In the way that she has constructed her inner world, she is simply not able to take in more food. Until this rigid and punitive attitude towards herself can be modified through a relationship, she cannot change this; this is precisely what she needs help with.

What we can ask her to do, however, is to undertake not to lose any more weight. This needs to be discussed carefully and the woman needs to think about the implications of it. From a therapeutic point of view, what needs to be established is that maintaining a weight which is safe is the responsibility of the woman herself. The therapist will be interested and concerned with her struggles to maintain her weight, but she cannot intervene in any practical way to affect it. This statement that the therapist will not control her is usually received by the anorexic with both relief and anxiety. She will not tolerate anyone trying to control her, but on the other hand there is a part of her which longs to be controlled and fed. If, during the course of therapy, her weight should fall to an unacceptably low level, this has to be discussed between therapist and client and a way found for the woman to get some help with her physical health. This is exactly the way a therapist would behave with any client whose psychological problems led to a deterioration in her physical health or who presented a special kind of risk. Interestingly, the vast majority of anorexic women do manage to hold their weight within the context of a therapeutic relationship. It is often a great relief for the woman to be told that her therapist is not expecting her to gain weight, merely to hold it and keep herself safe.

It is very important for therapist and client to be patient about weight increase. It is often one of the last things to change in the woman's life, but change it eventually will, when she is really ready. Many women who suffer from anorexia have felt under pressure all their lives to be more grown up and mature than they actually feel. They very often internalize this pressure and apply it to therapy, expecting themselves to 'get better' and put on weight before it really feels safe to do so. The therapist must avoid colluding with this and must uphold the woman's right to give up her defence at her own pace and in her own time. It is crucial that the defence is respected and seen as a way of coping – the only possible way of coping at the time.

Some therapists feel unable to judge whether or not it is safe to take an anorexic woman on for psychotherapy. She may look so thin and fragile and her weight seem so low by ordinary standards that the therapist feels she needs some independent opinion. It is perfectly possible to discuss with the woman the need to safeguard her health and, with her permission, to write to her family doctor for her or his advice. Most doctors are very happy to cooperate in this way and indeed often offer to monitor the woman's weight and physical health until it is more stable. This can be a useful way of taking any anxiety about weight and health out of the therapeutic situation and into a more appropriate one.

Many clients who want and need therapy have a physical condition related to their psychological difficulties which needs to be considered and managed in an appropriate way. The anorexic is no different in this respect, and it is helpful for therapists to remember this and not to allow their preconceptions about anorexia to cloud their perspective.

Bulimia

Bulimia and its physical consequences do not arouse as much anxiety as anorexia, mainly because the damage they cause is less visible. We have often noticed, too, that doctors are less inclined to be concerned about the physical effects of bingeing and purging than about the consequences of prolonged starvation. The problem with bulimia is that unlike anorexia it can have very dramatic and sudden consequences which are difficult to predict. Anorexia produces a gradual physical decline while bulimia can, exceptionally, produce a sudden crisis. While the majority of women who overeat and make themselves sick suffer little more than bad teeth and a chronically sore throat and mouth, women who abuse laxatives can deplete their bodies of essential elements which can occasionally precipitate heart failure or fits. In this sense it is rather like alcoholism, which generally runs a chronic course but which can occasionally make the sufferer severely ill.

A psychotherapist cannot in any real sense take responsibility for the health of a bulimic client, neither does it help for her to constantly remind the client of the damage she may be doing to herself. If the client wants information about such matters, she can be referred to an appropriate book. As with any self-destructive symptom, the client will at times feel great anxiety about what she is doing to herself, while at others she will simply bury her head in the sand.

If a therapist feels anxious about taking on a bulimic woman, it is perfectly reasonable to stipulate that she consult a doctor at least to find out about her state of health. While the client may initially protest about such a stipulation, it will often actually produce a sense of relief. The therapist is showing clearly that physical health, the body, is important and cannot be ignored. It may trigger the start of a recognition that the woman is a whole person and that it is not acceptable for her to abuse her body in order to deal with her feelings.

Compulsive eating

While compulsive eating does not usually produce symptoms

which are immediately life-threatening, there can be exceptions to this. Working with a diabetic who is a compulsive eater or a woman urgently in need of surgery which is being withheld because of her weight can make the therapist feel under great pressure to take control of the woman's eating and weight.

Of course, the compulsive eater herself consciously wishes to find someone to control her – that is why she is so often seduced into treatments which involve enforced dieting. Unconsciously, she will always undermine any attempts to control her and in our experience it is vital that the therapist confronts any feelings she may have of wanting the compulsive eater to lose weight in order to prove her a good therapist. She will come under immense pressure to take responsibility for all this and it is important that she is able to understand her own and her client's feelings and remain free to comment on what is being expected of her and what she is in fact able to offer.

The therapeutic relationship

The reason for going to some lengths to ensure that the client's health is safeguarded as far as possible is simply to allow the therapy to proceed without being dominated by this issue. It allows both client and therapist to proceed with some confidence. But beginning therapy is not easy.

There are very specific differences in approaching therapy with anorexics, bulimics and compulsive eaters, and some examples will be offered later in the chapter. What we can say, however, is that with all women with eating disorders, certain issues will always arise and will be important.

The compulsive eater often approaches therapy with little else consciously in mind except losing weight. She may well describe her preoccupation with food as 'silly', saying that there is really nothing wrong in her life and she cannot understand why she has such a painful addiction. She very much wants help – help to lose weight. The anorexic may present in a similar way, but denying that even her eating poses her with a problem. Although it is pitifully obvious to the observer that she is ill and emaciated, she may deny that this is anything more than a passing phase, which she now has firmly under control, and she expects to gain weight within the next week or two! The bulimic woman very often presents with a great deal of desperation. She feels tormented by her compulsive behaviour. She loathes what she does and yet she cannot stop herself. If only she could stop doing this, she is sure that everything in her life would be fine. And yet she knows she will go on doing it.

These different ways of presenting at the beginning of therapy give a good indication of the underlying problem, which is precisely the same in each case but which is dealt with so differently. All these women have the utmost difficulty in knowing what they need or want. The compulsive eater knows that she needs and wants help. Like food, she craves it. But she cannot let herself know what she really needs help with. She has no sense that it is her feelings which are giving her such trouble. This mirrors the way she manages her life. Instead of knowing what she wants in life, she only knows she wants food. When it comes to therapy, all she can be aware of is wanting to lose weight.

The anorexic initially cannot allow herself to take in anything from the therapy. She feels she truly does not need anything, the same as she feels about food. The bulimic woman does feel her own desperation, but at the same time has no belief that it can be made more bearable. She eats and eats, but knows that she must not let it nourish her. The task of therapy in these early days is to show the woman how her eating reflects and mirrors her attitude to herself and her life and to examine the way it manifests itself in the therapy relationship. In other words, we are seeking to broaden the woman's interest so that she can think about more than just her symptom. By beginning with the symptom, we can start to help the woman decode it and find her interest in her whole self.

Therapy in process

The emergence of the little girl

During the course of therapy with a woman with an eating disorder, at some point the little girl whose needs have for so long been denied will begin to make herself felt. Just how and when this comes about will depend on the actual circumstances under which the original repression of that childlike part of the self took place.

This childlike part of the self feels so horrible and frightening to the woman that she is usually really anxious about getting to know it. We can understand the role of the therapist as making a gradual reintroduction of the hurt and furious child to the adult woman. For very many women, as we have seen, the period of time in which they could really experience their dependence in a positive way has been cut short. For Diana, life changed dramatically when she was four years old. The family moved from their home in the Caribbean as immigrants to the UK. They were full of hopeful expectations but found themselves in a land which was overtly racist and hostile. A year later her younger brother was born, her mother suffered a serious physical illness and her father began to show signs of alcoholism. The little girl quickly learnt to hide the vulnerable, frightened and needy part of herself, as well as her furious jealousy at the birth of the baby. No one had time to deal with or even notice what was happening to her. Throughout her childhood Diana became more and more competent and compliant, and as her family life deteriorated she showed a remarkably grown-up capacity for taking care of herself and her brother. When she was fifteen she began to show signs of acute anxiety and depression and eventually developed a very severe anorexic episode. She partially recovered from this and went on to have an outstandingly successful academic and later professional career. However, she was still unable to make relationships, to have or to do anything creative, and she found herself constantly terrified of her own feelings, which her eating disorder enabled her cruelly to repress. When she entered therapy, Diana was a successful editor in a publishing company. She managed her working life with great efficiency. The 'grown-up' part of her was highly developed and successfully hid the frightened little girl.

In her therapy, Diana could at first do no more than talk about her past. Along with the therapist she could begin to understand how she must have felt as a child, but she could not feel the child-like part of herself which remained split off and unacknowledged in the present. Whenever she did become aware of the actual feelings she had experienced as a child, Diana found them almost unbearable. It was not only her profound sense of loneliness, confusion and anger which terrified her, but also a sense that no one would be able or prepared to tolerate these feelings. Often at first she would implore the therapist to take her disturbing feelings away, but gradually, sensing that the therapist could sit with her in a sympathetic way without panicking at her distress, she came to find the distressed part of herself more bearable.

The response of the adult

We have to remember that eating disorders develop in order to hide and protect the needy, chaotic, childlike part of the self. As that begins to emerge, so simultaneously do the 'adult' defences which have been concealing it. This part of the personality is not in fact adult at all. It is a kind of false adult which has come into being to repress the more spontaneous, needy, dependent part of the self. In fact it is a helpless defence, which cannot in the least enable the woman to look after herself. Its only solution to stress or crisis is to refuse, punish, induce guilt and simply say 'no' to the woman's own needs.

As Christine became more aware of some of her real feelings during the course of her therapy, she found that she wanted and needed all kinds of foods which she had forbidden herself. She wanted sweet food, puddings, baby foods, ice cream and cake. She was so terrified of these longings that she forbade herself anything but the plainest and most unpalatable of foods. However, the newly discovered needy part of her rejected these and became furious and for a while, whenever she thought about what she should eat, she felt a helpless rage and could eat nothing. Here we can clearly see the way in which conflicting wishes, needs and parts of the self are shown and played out through food. What Christine and her therapist also had to confront was the cruelty and ferocity with which the 'adult' part of her abused the hidden little girl.

The greatest fear at this stage in the therapy is of the chaos and confusion which the woman feels lies beneath her eating disorder. This sense of chaos often expresses itself through chaotic eating. The anorexic woman may find herself driven to the binges she most fears; the compulsive eater and the bulimic woman may find that their eating patterns become even more bizarre and frightening. This is actually an externalizing of the internal chaos, which consists of the woman's own chaotic feelings and her reaction to them. For her, everything which disturbs the smooth surface of her existence signals chaos; every feeling which is not within her control threatens to overwhelm her. It is only through the sustained ability of the therapist to tolerate this messy, chaotic aspect of the woman's experience that she is able to come to know it and integrate it herself.

Ways of working

The aim of therapy is to enable the woman with an eating disorder to look beneath the defence of her own symptoms and to find a more settled relationship with what lies beneath. The aim is not to push or force her to give up her defensive symptoms before she is ready to do so. This means that while taking every opportunity of using what she says and what she does to reveal to her the part of herself she doesn't want to know about, the therapist has to understand and communicate her understanding of the defences as ways of coping which are related to the individual personal experience of the woman. These coping defences are also directly related to the experience of all women in our society, but though it is essential for the therapist to understand this, it is not helpful for her to talk about her client's experience in terms of the experience of women in general. For the woman herself, it is her experience which matters. She may well prefer to spend her sessions discussing the politics of gender relations, but if she does so, she will be no more prepared than she was before to be in touch with the needy little girl inside *her*, who goes back long before the time when the adult could understand the social and political issues involved.

Given that the client is trying hard to conceal the needy, dependent, childlike part of herself, she is bound to find it hard to show her therapist that aspect of her personality. The great danger is that she will come along, almost like a second therapist, to discuss this difficult part of herself which causes her so much pain while the struggling, voiceless child continues to produce the symptoms. Often it is through issues which seem peripheral to the therapy, the issues around the edges, that the real distress can emerge. The holidays which the therapist takes, the breaks in the therapy, can sometimes provide an indication of the woman's real needs, which she cannot even feel, let alone express, while the therapy continues uninterrupted. All the time the therapist is there the woman can keep her dependence under control. She may not be demanding, she may in fact be the 'ideal' client. But perhaps when the therapist is not there, she will actually come into touch with the part of herself which feels let down, abandoned and furious.

We have found that running time-limited groups with bulimic women can provide just this opportunity. The experience of having something which is good and valuable but which, by its very nature, is limited can enable women to feel the sense of outrage about not having been given enough which for so long they have denied. Bulimic women very often express their ambivalence about their own needs by the way they deal with their therapy. Sometimes this ambivalence will show itself by the woman missing certain sessions. Hilary was able to use her therapy well and to make considerable improvement. She talked about her attempts to resist the pressures of her family, to discover more about her own needs and wishes, and for much of the time she felt a new sense of enthusiasm and potential growth. She also spoke of certain times when an angry, desperate and despairing cloud would descend on her and she could think of nothing else to do but to eat and make herself sick. She had a pattern of missing certain sessions. She would always have a very good reason; illness, the unexpected demands of work, a problem with her car. It was only when the therapist questioned these missed sessions and explored what this pattern really meant that it emerged that the times when she was absent from her therapy were precisely the times when she was feeling so desperate. Instead of bringing that angry, despairing part of herself to her therapy, she was dealing with it alone and in secret via her symptom. Hilary could not believe that anyone would be prepared to help that part of her. She had continued in her relationship with her therapist the pattern established with her family, whereby only the happy, lively, enthusiastic part of her was acceptable. She felt secretly furious with the therapist for not giving her the help she needed, but always managed to vomit up her anger before coming to her session.

Coming late or early to sessions can also be the only way the woman can find of expressing a part of herself which is being left out of the therapy. It is particularly important for the therapist to protect the boundaries of the therapy, to ensure that sessions begin and end on time and to be alert to the meanings of any attempts to alter or cross these boundaries. In a time-limited group for bulimic women, the therapists in one of the early sessions finished the group on time and left the room. They later discovered that the women had remained in the room, continuing the 'group' for a considerable time after they had left. At the next session they raised this as an issue for the group and suggested that it represented a wish on the part of the group to have more time than the therapists were offering. They also made it clear that it was not possible for the group to continue the session after the time was up. The group responded with mild surprise that the therapists should make so much fuss about something so trivial. The women were quite unable to acknowledge that their actions had any significance.

The following week, the therapists arrived at the time the group should begin only to find that all the women had been there for some time and that the group had already started! This was interpreted as the group's attempts to tell the therapists how angry and disappointed they were feeling with the little bit of attention they were receiving and also as an assertion of independence. The women were clearly telling the therapists that they could look after each other and did not need what the therapists had to offer. This time the group responded with fury. How dare the therapists try to dictate how much time they spent together? Clearly the therapists did not really care about them, did not worry about how upset they might feel, did not really understand how much help they needed. The therapists were accused of trying to control them to protect their own position as leaders of the group.

All these feelings were carefully discussed and analysed. They had in fact been around in the group for some time, but instead of being put into words in the group they had been acted out around the edges. Many of the women could feel echoes of the past in their present feelings about the therapists. They recounted painful moments when their parents had seemed more concerned with creating the appearance of a happy family than with really understanding their daughter's needs; times when they had felt in need of far more help and care than they were getting and knew that they could not protest or complain; situations in which their real feelings had been called childish and inappropriate and they had been told to go away and come back when they were feeling better. These were the most difficult feelings for the women in this group to acknowledge, but also the most important. Time and again we see how these hidden feelings, left over from childhood, representing a part of the woman of which she feels ashamed, come to the surface around issues to do with boundaries.

In other time-limited groups, we have often found that very important feelings come up around the ending of the group time. Indeed, in some groups the issue of ending dominates almost from the start. It can feel so terrifying to know that care, attention and nurturing is limited and will come to an end that it can seem better not to have any at all. This of course is graphically represented by the anorexic, who would rather have none of her needs met than suffer the pain and humiliation of being left still wanting more.

Every woman with an eating disorder has her own unique history, her store of experiences and her particular hidden troubled feelings. The principle underlying what we have said about a therapeutic response is that all of these feelings need to be brought to life, experienced, understood and worked through in relation to the therapist.

The choice of group or individual therapy

Wherever possible, we feel that the decision about whether therapy is one-to-one or in a group should be a matter of personal choice for the client. (Here we are talking about therapist-led groups, rather than self-help groups, which are discussed at length in the following two chapters.) We very often find that anorexic women do not choose to be members of a group, but prefer to work at making an individual relationship. We have, however, seen anorexic women do well in groups where people come with a variety of problems and symptoms – not just eating disorders.

We have led a number of groups for bulimic women, in which all the women had the same or similar symptoms. This method of treatment has the great advantage of feeling safe, and the sense of being able to reveal a hidden part of the self cannot be overstated. At present, we would probably be inclined to say that a group is the treatment likely to be most helpful for bulimic women, but again, wherever possible, the woman herself should be given the choice.

Working in institutions

A number of therapists who come to the Women's Therapy Centre for supervision of their work are themselves working in hospitals. Their original training may be in nursing, medicine, occupational therapy, social work, psychology or dietetics. Many of these professional people are struggling to do a good job but find themselves in a somewhat difficult position in terms of the institution and their own roles within it. It is our view that most women with eating disorders are best treated outside of in-patient settings. Nonetheless, many are treated in hospitals and the quality of treatment they receive is vitally important.

For therapists working within these settings, one of the most difficult problems is the very powerful and conflicting feelings which women with eating disorders arouse in the team who care for them. Anorexic and bulimic women – who often do find themselves in hospitals – can create splits and divisions within a nursing group or a multi-disciplinary team, perhaps more than any other group of patients. It is important to realize that these conflicting feelings are the projections by the woman herself of her own conflicts and dilemmas. For one member of the team the woman appears as a hurt child, needing sympathy and understanding. To another she may seem manipulative and self-centred. The important point is that both of these responses are reactions to the woman's feelings about herself, disowned and projected on to her helpers.

There is no simple way to deal with this situation. It is actually easier if there is only one therapist, but for those therapists who find themselves as members of a team, the way forward is to acknowledge that everyone's responses to the woman are legitimate and valuable, yet none of them has the whole story. The whole range of feeling responses represents the way the woman has come to feel about herself and the responses she has elicited from people close to her in the past. It is on the basis of this shared and accepted range of reactions that the therapeutic team must decide upon and agree a response.

10
PRINCIPLES OF SELF-HELP

This chapter, about the general principles of running self-help groups for eating disorders, is based on our experience at the Women's Therapy Centre. There are differences between running self-help groups for compulsive eaters, for bulimics and for anorexics, though there are also many points of similarity. In this chapter, we attempt to make clear the underlying principles of self-help, as well as articulating differences which need to be borne in mind by women with different sorts of problems.

Many of the groups set up at the Women's Therapy Centre are based on self-help principles. The Centre has been running and organizing self-help groups for compulsive eaters for more than a decade, and in more recent years the self-help principle has also been applied to other problems, such as bulimia and anorexia.

Self-help for eating disorders is quite unlike other more traditional forms of treatment, in which the woman is supposed to be 'cured' of her eating problem without reference to her own wants and needs and indeed without understanding the causes of her problem. In the more traditional situation, she comes to the 'specialist' who knows what is best for her, what her normal or ideal weight should be, what size and shape she has to acquire. In the worst instances, she is given a diet sheet with a short lecture on how important losing or gaining weight is to her health and well-being, and there is no attempt either to understand the reason or to work with her on any aspect of her problem other than losing or gaining weight.

The self-help model assumes that these women had a very good reason at some point in their lives to 'choose' (unconsciously) that kind of behaviour and to use food as they do. This kind of thinking further contends that no one just gives up their defences without understanding what they are defending and how they can do it differently. We believe that this is the basis of the therapy used in these groups.

There is an important issue about motivation in finding a solution to eating problems, and it is very often linked with control. Women who suffer from eating disorders very often *are* reluctant to seek help. One of the reasons for this is the fear that asking for help will result in their lives being taken over and controlled by experts, and, regrettably, these fears are sometimes borne out in reality. Women who have never felt able to ask for help and many more who have had unsatisfactory experiences of professional help have felt able to join a self-help group.

Sometimes, a self-help group can be the first step towards finding and accepting professional help. With the support of the group, a woman may be able to look at and overcome her resistance to seeking the kind of help she needs. In other cases, a woman may have already used professional help to make some progress with her problem. She may then use the group primarily to help her make the kind of changes in her life as well as in her eating which giving up the symptom implies. We use a self-help approach for compulsive eating groups at the Centre because we believe that this allows the woman to give respect to herself, with the aid of other women who have the same problem, so she can find *her own* conflicts, *her own* underlying reasons, without relying on others to give her the answer.

In many ways, it is a difficult way of working. There are no external impositions about eating; no diet sheets, no rules about what and when to eat. There are a few rules to give structure to the groups and to allow the participants to learn to set their boundaries in a helpful way, but all external understandings about calories, weight, good/bad, allowed/forbidden are not relevant and this is the reason why the groups are self-help. Women help each other and themselves, not guided by external advice and instructions as to the nature of their problem or, more importantly, as to the nature of the 'cure' for it.

In describing our own experiences of self-help, we hope to be able to point to some of the processes which can occur and which are helpful. We do not want to set out prescriptions for self-help. Each individual and each group is different and the suggestions we make should be taken as a starting point from which groups can use their own creativity. Above all, we would encourage self-help groups to ground all their work in the experience of their own members rather than trying to make women's lives fit any particular view or theory.

It may be helpful to start with describing what our experience tells us is the best way of working with each one of these problems; this may also say something about the nature of the problem itself.

We have found self-help groups to be most helpful for compulsive eaters. It is important to understand that compulsive eaters do acknowledge that they need *something*. They do not always know what it is, and often they will turn to food instead of finding out what that need may be. They may need time to regain the capacity to find out about their needs, but at least they acknowledge that they exist underneath the urge to overeat.

Anorexics, on the other hand, believe that they are beyond needs, that they have none. If we imagine, therefore, a group of women all saying, 'I do not need anything from anyone, not even this group (or maybe especially not from this group),' it will be difficult to imagine that the group will go very far and it may end up being rendered useless. The Eating Disorders Association (formerly Anorexic Aid) is a national charity which has for many years coordinated a network of self-help groups for anorexics. The success of these groups lies in the fact that the contacts, the women who initiate and take responsibility for the group, are themselves generally recovered, or well on the road to recovery. In addition, they are always urged to seek the help and guidance of a counsellor who can advise and support the contact. This, we believe, is an important key to success in self-help groups for anorexics. It is very important to have someone in the group (and preferably more than one person) who is further along the way to recovery and thus more in touch with feelings which other group members may deny.

It must be acknowledged, though, that some women in an anorexic episode or phase simply cannot use self-help in the early stages. They are likely to be helped much more by patient one-to-one counselling or therapy, with the offer of joining a group at a later stage.

For bulimic women we have found that the most helpful way of working is a one-year group, led by a therapist. This is because they probably acknowledge their needs but at the same time try to deny and negate them. The acknowledgement of this ambivalence is an important stage of working through the problem, and until it can be acknowledged and felt, it is likely to be enacted in the group. A therapist is able to point out this enactment and therefore make it possible for women to continue to use the group.

Many bulimic women do not have the option of a therapist-led group. We will therefore offer suggestions for self-help bulimia groups, and we know of several such groups which have been very successful.

Some general principles of working in self-help groups

(You will find many more in *In Our Own Hands*[1] and in *Fat is a Feminist Issue*.[2])

Time-sharing

Time-sharing is a very important issue in a compulsive eating self-help group. Women who think of themselves as 'greedy' (which is the case for most compulsive eaters) might feel very reluctant to take up the group's time. We have also learnt that the women who seem to have least to say may be able to make a very helpful contribution to the group if they are given the opportunity to do so, and if not encouraged they feel shy or frightened to make these contributions. It is therefore a good idea to structure the groups so that there is an expectation that everyone will say something about the particular issue or theme which is dealt with at any given session. On the other hand, it is important to leave some unstructured time (time where women speak if they so choose and say nothing if they do not want to speak), which can be used by those women who feel that a particular area of work has a special meaning for them, or for any other issues which have come up for them during the week.

One way of achieving this is to allocate, for instance, half the time (maybe an hour) to a time-shared theme (sixty minutes divided by the number of women in the group), leaving the second half for a more general discussion of the issues that arise for each individual in the group. It is useful to appoint a time-keeper, who keeps an eye on the watch and indicates to women when their allocated time is up. It is good to have a different woman time-keeping at each session, so that you share responsibilities as equally as possible.

Meeting place

It is best for members of the group to rotate meeting in each other's homes. Ideally the members will live near each other, as travelling long distances can sometimes become a reason and excuse to leave the group when things in the group become difficult. When some feelings become unbearable it could unconsciously become connected with the effort made to get to the group and present a good excuse to stop coming. Rotating meetings in homes in the same area is easy, and is important, especially in order that different women take responsibility at different sessions. In this way no one woman in the group feels that she is the 'regular' hostess of the group and hence a sort of responsible leader.

If one woman in a group does decide to take overall responsibility for convening the group (as happens successfully in some anorexia groups), it is advisable to try to find premises away from her home for the group to meet in. The group should share the cost involved in hiring a room.

Themes

Before a meeting it is important to arrange a theme, exercise or something to work on. This can be done either by preparing a plan for a few sessions in advance, or by leaving a few minutes at the end of every meeting to discuss the plan for the next week. In the next chapter we have some suggestions for possible themes and ways of working on them. However, it is not constructive for the session to start with members not knowing what they are going to talk about and searching for a theme at the beginning of the group. It is also good for the group members to arrange the sessions so that there is a sense of progression from one theme to another, where the 'easier' subjects to talk about come at the first few sessions until the trust is built to discuss the more difficult, frightening subjects.

Socializing

The group should be aware that they should not allow the sessions to become a social situation, where the members meet to chat to each other about what has happened during the last few days. Some rules that may help you are:

- All members make a commitment to come to every session and to come on time.
- If one woman cannot come to a session, she should notify the group in advance. If something urgent comes up at the last minute she should phone the person in whose house that session is to be held so that the rest of the group will not wait for her.
- The group should start exactly on time, and if people want coffee or tea before the group, they can come a bit earlier. In this way, the length of the session ($2-2\frac{1}{2}$ hours) will be used fully for 'work'. If women want to have social interactions they should do so outside group time. However, this in itself can create some problems – if some members meet socially and not others, it may set up a situation whereby those who do not meet outside the group feel excluded and those who do meet may pair up and become a powerful unit in the group, seeming exclusive to other members. The group must be aware of all these issues when considering social contact outside the group. Whether members decide to have social contact or not, it is always important not to talk about the group issues or other group members or feelings about the group.

Confidentiality

At the beginning of the group, confidentiality must be stressed. Some groups will take place in rural areas where people know each other. It is not possible to trust the group and to be open in it unless a commitment is made to keep all that happens within the group confidential. Also, as we mentioned above, members should not discuss what happens in sessions outside of the group, not even with other members, because a rule of confidentiality is vital to keep the group safe.

Feelings

Talking about the themes connected with eating disorders and the experiences related to them can be very difficult and bring up many different feelings, often ones which are hidden from ordinary consciousness, feelings which are difficult to bear and which we may not be so used to expressing or seeing others express. Our experience in groups is that often, when a woman talks about painful feelings and starts crying, for instance, the rest of the women, not knowing what to do, feel uneasy, maybe confused, perhaps identifying with her or trying to comfort her. A woman crying can bring painful and uncomfortable feelings to the rest of the group. However, it is very important for the woman to stay with her feelings, with the support of the group. It is important for her to know that her crying, her pain, are acceptable, that they are not something other people reject or want to comfort away. She needs to know that other people can bear with her when she is in pain, and she may then realize that it is not such an unacceptable feeling, it need not be denied, cut off, pushed aside. The group is a good and safe place to experiment with these feelings, and with the fears of expressing and experiencing them, and to find out that other people can accept them.

As we usually find indirect ways to deal with these difficult feelings (one of the ways is through symptoms connected with food), it is vital to be able to stay with these feelings and not simply to comfort them away.

Leaving the group

Sometimes women who have been in a group for only a few weeks or so stop overeating or vomiting, feel they have solved the problem, and want to leave the group. It is not impossible for such a thing to happen so quickly, but please allow yourself to stay with the group for longer than this, as it is highly unlikely that a problem that has been with you for some considerable time will disappear overnight.

The same applies to women who, feeling that they have been in the group for a long time and that nothing has happened, want to give up. Working on eating disorders is long and hard work. You must give yourself time both to gain understanding of your problems and to be able to use it to change your behaviour and establish a new pattern for yourself. If you feel you want to leave right at the start of the group, or after a while when you feel that not much has shifted in your eating patterns, give yourself time in the group to work on it. Research into self-help groups by Parry-Crooke and Ryan has shown that several groups have disintegrated because people have left early.[3] One of the ways they suggest for dealing with this problem is to have the group set up on the basis of a time limit – say, nine months – and then if necessary to decide to prolong the group. This way members of the group know in advance what the initial contract is and do not feel that they have to wait for ever to leave the group.

What are group dynamics?

Sheila Ernst, in an unpublished paper on group dynamics in women's groups, claims that whatever happens in a group will often reflect the context within which the group exists. Thus in a mixed group of men and women, or black and white people, or middle- and working-class people, modes of relating may emerge which are clearly socially linked. The group, whether deliberately set up as a therapy group or collected around work, begins to function in ways which are not explicable purely in terms of the individuals who comprise it.

The process of projection is particularly important. By this we mean the process whereby group members push out and get rid of certain thoughts, feelings and characteristics of themselves which they hate and cannot acknowledge. These are denied in the self, but perceived and responded to as characteristics of other members of the group. Individuals are like points in a social network; processes will go on within the individual, but also between individuals and within the whole group. Thus the group may 'resonate' to a theme – or a group member may quite unconsciously project aspects of herself which she cannot tolerate into other group members, or into a sub-group. Sometimes, the whole group will seem to locate certain features or aspects of personality in one person (scapegoating), but what is often happening is that the scapegoat is carrying the whole group's denied anger or envy or desire to be dependent. Sometimes a group can come to represent an individual's family or part of the family.

Projections of this nature – where another individual is invested with very powerful emotional connotations which may or may not relate to how the person really is – may make it more difficult for the group to carry out its tasks. Understanding the unconscious projections may help group members to relate more effectively in the adult here and now.

Basic assumption groups: Another way of looking at what happens in groups focuses on the way groups defend themselves against the frightening experience of being in a group. Bion[4] suggests that there are three basic patterns of defence which operate to protect the group against pain but also may prevent it from pursuing its task effectively.

Dependence: Group members are stuck in their longing to be looked after, and operate as if certain individuals in the group will parent them, thus avoiding taking responsibility for themselves.

Fight and flight: Group members deal with a painful or difficult situation by quarrelling and 'running away'.

Pairing: To avoid dealing with what is happening in the group individuals pair up and have a special relationship, often gossiping about the rest of the group from a safe position.

Making a group safe

To create a situation where the whole group can feel safe enough to work together and to allow change and development to take place, it is vital to create a safe setting. In a therapy group great emphasis is placed on the group leader (facilitator) being responsible for this. In self-help groups it must be done through creating safe boundaries for the group. Clear boundaries need to be set (this can be done by the whole group), and what is and is not acceptable behaviour must be defined. Then it becomes possible for individuals to re-own their projections and to understand when splitting or scapegoating is taking place.

Women's groups

Sheila Ernst suggests that in a women's group the issue of dependence is often central, with a conflict between the fear of depending and the longing to be dependent. Women, afraid of intimacy and feeling needy, may try to deal with their needs by caring (or attempting to care) for others. They may also link together, finding common ground, and define 'bad' people (often men or mothers) as being outside the group. On one level this reflects their experience – on another it prevents the women from exploring their differences, and their own power and strengths. For instance, a group of compulsive eaters got on very well as long as none of them lost any weight – it began to be clear that some of the women were afraid of overcoming their eating problems lest they got thinner than others in the group, thus becoming 'different'.

Setting clear boundaries is particularly important for women, who generally have difficulty in setting limits and boundaries; this is especially true for women who are compulsive eaters.

Within a clear structure we can learn to be aware of the kinds of group processes described above, to recognize some of the defensive strategies which groups adopt. These processes which take place within a group can be destructive both to the individuals involved and to the group as a whole, which may not be able to sustain itself but may break up. However, the group also has the potential to be a supportive, constructive and healing environment.

On the basis of understanding more about group dynamics and having some clues as to how to work with them, the group members may now find it easier to decide how often they want a session to work on what is going on in the group. We suggest every sixth session, but we realize that each group will have different needs and a different pace, and will need to decide among themselves.

It should also be noted that these compulsive eating self-help groups have a task, and that group dynamics is not the focus of the group but just a way not to clog the path towards this task; it should not take the place of the task itself, which is to work on issues of compulsive eating and its connections to every individual's life.

Results of research

We have been fortunate in having available some detailed research on the self-help compulsive eating groups set up at the Women's Therapy Centre. This research was carried out by Joanna Ryan and Georgie Parry-Crooke and was funded by the Health Education Council.[5] One of the main recommendations was that the group should be given help in working with its own dynamics.

It is quite evident now – both from the findings of the research and from reports we receive from our group leaders who set the self-help groups up – that special attention must be given to this aspect of the group in a regular and structured way rather than in a point of crisis when members find it more difficult to sort things out.

Our compulsive eating groups are structured on the model suggested in Susie Orbach's *Fat is a Feminist Issue*. One model we use for these groups is that of two initial meetings with a leader in which women explore central issues concerning their eating habits – their feelings about food and their bodies – and other subjects that arise and are common to all compulsive eating groups. After these two sessions, the group progresses as a self-help group. The leader who started the group will do one follow-up session, which will take place two to three months after the first meeting. In this follow-up session members have the opportunity, with the help of the leader, to look at problems that have arisen for them both as a group and as individuals in the group. After the follow-up session, the group goes its own way with an open invitation to ask the Centre for help with any problems that come up for them over the following months. In reality, self-help groups have tended to under-use this resource. This may stem from the fact that compulsive eaters often have difficulty in asking for specific help for themselves. They may feel that their problem is not serious enough to call upon the 'mother organization', or they may deny altogether that they have a problem in the group and may need external help with it. This can sometimes deter groups from contacting the Centre to ask for help, and since this has often been the case, what tends to happen is that the groups dissolve or dwindle or sometimes ask for help when it is too late.

In our long experience we have found that this structure of two sessions with a leader allows the women in the groups to get an experience of our approach, to see what it is all about, and to work out what specific directions they can take according to the analysis of their own weight history, without becoming dependent on the leader to 'do it for them'. The leader is there to explain, to show, to initiate, but not to take over each woman's responsibility, hard work or exploration from her. In groups which are led for a longer period of time, women often come expecting the therapist to give them a magic solution to 'do it for them' in some way or another. This expectation is not always conscious but is most likely to be there, especially if the therapist is with the group for some time. It is always a very important and central theme in the group for quite a while, and once the members of the group acknowledge that it is not going to happen and that they really have to 'do it for themselves', a great many feelings come up, including anger and disappointment as well as hope. In a structure which has only two sessions with a leader this is not going to be such an important issue, because there is not enough time for this dependence and expectation to develop, and the promise which women project on to the leader is not so immediate. However, the issue of wanting a magic solution, someone to 'do it for them' is still going to be present and needs to be worked through. These two sessions are a long enough time to learn, but not long enough to become dependent and develop particular expectations, and they provide someone to turn to in case of difficulty or despair.

How to set up a group

If there is not already a group in your area and you wish to set one up, you can start a group yourself. We would like to give you every encouragement. We know that the idea sounds quite off-putting, and you may think: 'I've never done anything like it: I would never be able to do it.' We cannot say that it is easy, but we can say that many women who once thought and felt as you do have tried and succeeded. This very step in itself could be very valuable as a way to assert your needs, to make yourself powerful, to initiate a project to help yourself and others. If you know a woman living near you who suffers with the same problem, you may find it easier to combine resources and share the problems and responsibilities of taking the first step together.

You can start by placing a note in the local press or on a

Principles of Self-help

local notice board, asking women to contact you if they are interested in a self-help group. From experience, we have learnt that travelling long distances can be an obstacle after the initial excitement of the first few meetings, so try to find women who live quite near you.

After finding enough women who are interested in a group (a good number is about seven, but groups can be formed with more or fewer), try to find an evening that suits you all, and a place in which you can meet for two to three hours. Perhaps you could meet in a different member's house each week.

You may not be able to find enough women to form a group, but even two women meeting together can be very helpful to each other if they really commit themselves to meeting every week on a regular basis, without turning it into a social occasion but really getting down to discussing the issues and working on their problems. At the first session you could begin by getting to know one another, talking about your history of compulsive eating and going on from there to some fantasy work and exercises concerning your problem. Some suggestions for issues to work on and ways to proceed are listed in the next chapter.

In our groups on compulsive eating, we work on two levels. One is the conscious and unconscious meaning of being, or feeling, overweight, and the other level is to do with our relationship to food. The first could be defined as psychological exploration, as it is more to do with the woman's internal world, her feelings about herself, often an unconscious aspect of her. The second will be partly defined as behavioural, as it deals with re-learning, re-educating oneself about eating habits and patterns, about listening to one's body, about giving oneself respect and attention in relation to eating.

In the way we work, every woman in the group will try to find the specific meaning, or combination of meanings, that being fat has for *her*, in the picture she has of her life. We will be describing some exercises later which we suggest will help her to do this. We will also describe later some ways of working on the second level, that of each woman's relationship to food.

Aims of compulsive eating groups

As we have seen, at the very basis of this eating behaviour is a conflict that the woman who eats compulsively is trying to deal with by overeating, by being obsessed with food, and by becoming overweight or feeling overweight. The eating habits and being fat are facets of an attempt either to block the conscious or unconscious conflicts that lie beneath them or to deal with them in an indirect way. The aim of the therapy is not to solve or resolve the conflicts, but to bring them to the surface, to consciousness, to get to know what the conflicts are, where they come from, what fears and fantasies are involved, and to learn the details of the conflicts so that the women can experience them directly. The fantasies can then be checked out in the environment, in real life, and the fears can be experienced and dealt with in a direct way.

To make this statement clearer we can give an example. Often, as well as finding a protection in the fat and having an unconscious fear of being thin, the woman has a fear of being promiscuous, and the fat can protect her from this fear. She may believe somewhere inside her that every man will want her if she is thin, and that she will be unable to say 'no' to these advances towards her. The first step of her work in the group will be to understand the fear and bring it to consciousness; for her to acknowledge, to become conscious of, the fact that she is afraid of her own promiscuity and sexuality and also of others' sexuality in relation to her. The next step is to check out the reality – is it true that every time a man makes a pass at her she has to say 'yes'? Is she able to refuse? If not, how can she deal with that in a direct way? How can she learn to know what she wants and say yes to that and refuse what she doesn't want, which includes her knowledge of herself in relation to food, people, events, sexuality and everything else?

The main purpose of the therapy is thus, as a first step, to make conscious the unconscious motivations of the compulsive eater, and then to learn ways to separate what the fat is doing in fantasy from the purpose it is serving in reality; to separate the qualities that belong to the fat from the ones that have been imposed upon it; to learn to say in words and deliver the messages that the fat is giving; to understand what are the statements made by the fat and slowly learn to say it in words, not in hidden messages. The purpose is further to understand what fears are involved in being thin, what investments have been made in being fat, and again to separate and deal with the fears and the

Principles of Self-help

investments in a clear and direct way. The point is to recognize that being thin is simply a body size rather than a world of utter happiness. Through therapy, the realization comes that one is in essence the same person, fat or thin. One doesn't gain a sense of humour by losing a few pounds, or become more able to relate to people warmly by gaining a few. One is either warm or cold or both, but no one is like that because of being fat or thin or could change to any of these through losing or gaining weight.

Another aim, through understanding her self-disgust and low self-image and in the warm, safe and supportive atmosphere that it is hoped the group will become, is to learn to give more to herself, to allow herself more respect and assertiveness and to get to like and accept herself more as she is *now*, rather than constantly living in expectation of future transformation. To live for the moment, not a life postponed until that day when she will be her ideal size.

Another important aim of the group is to create a supportive and warm environment where women will be able to talk about the very painful and shameful areas connected with their compulsive eating. Obviously this aim is important for any therapy group, but for the compulsive eater there is so much secrecy and shame involved that the issue of trust and openness becomes even more important, to the point where many women feel relieved just to have the possibility of sharing their eating patterns with other women in the same situation. So there is always an initial feeling of euphoria when a woman finds out that she is not the only one in the world behaving in such a way, that she is not a total freak. In the research it was found out that this support and sense of identification is one of the vital strengths of the group, and is what women feel they gain from it. It creates closeness and trust and allows women to feel safe, identified with each other, supported, not isolated, and confirmed about who they are and their struggles in relation to it.

On another level is the aim of working on behaviour – looking very carefully at when each woman feels like overeating, what the events are that precede a binge, what emotions are involved and what the main issues are that give rise to this urge to stuff herself. What are her patterns of eating? Does she eat standing up? Sitting? Walking in the streets? How much respect and attention does she devote to her food and to eating? Each woman must constantly look at her behaviour in order to find out the connections. She must try and look at what she wants to say when she eats compulsively, what the message is that she is trying to convey, who she is speaking to and what ways she can find to convey the message without doing it through eating. What other ways are there to treat herself? What are the things she enjoys doing? What are the things she is inhibited from doing by her fatness?

Another important aim is to find out what the woman likes, what she wants and what she needs, and to try to separate these from what she actually takes in, whether from not knowing what she really wants, not daring to ask for or take it, or feeling that she does not deserve it. She must learn to accept herself with her positive and negative sides and to stop believing that she must be perfect – hence feeling desperation when she sees that she is not. Learning to own her fat and see her body as a whole is an important part of the therapy. One can never get rid of something that one feels does not belong to one. It is only through owning it and accepting it as part of her that the woman can start to be able to let go of it.

Aims of anorexia groups

As we mentioned earlier, it is often said that anorexic women have a lot of difficulty in working in groups, especially self-help groups, because of their insistence on not having any needs and their difficulties in taking anything in. That includes care and nourishment of any kind, and the group will of course come into this category. Therefore a group of women who strongly deny their need for each other and for the group will have a difficult task to share, care and nourish one another. However, Anorexic Aid (now renamed the Eating Disorders Association) has many years of experience of successfully setting up and running groups for anorexic women and their families. Before taking any further steps, we strongly suggest you contact them. Notwithstanding the difficulties, we here suggest some practical applications based on our understanding of anorexia.

In anorexia, as in compulsive eating, at the very heart of the behaviour lies a conflict that the anorexic woman is trying to deal with indirectly through being obsessed with food, preventing herself from eating and being underweight. The aim of the group will be, therefore, not to solve or resolve the conflict, but to bring it into consciousness, to get to a detailed understanding of its origins and to point to where it became unbearable and had to be diverted to a defensive pattern which was expressed in anorexia. Bringing the fears and fantasies to the surface and knowing the 'areas' they are related to (sexuality, relationships, etc.) will allow the woman to deal with the conflict in a more direct, authentic way than through starvation, denial, thinness and rituals around food and eating. For example, with a conflict around femininity – the wish to look like a little girl or a boy – one has to work with what this conflict is, what the fear is of being a woman, what womanhood and femininity mean, what menstruation symbolizes, etc., and then look at whether these fears could be dealt with in a different way and what real choices one has around womanhood and femininity.

We must look at what purpose is served by the obsession with preventing oneself from eating, the obsession with rules, regulations and routine with food. What do all these obsessions and preoccupations of thought and action do for the woman in her current life? What do they cause her to do and what do they prevent her from doing? What kind of life-style does she lead, and how is it different from what her life would be like without them? For example, had she not been underweight would she still have the same circle of friends? The same job? The same life-style? She must look at her current life and recognize the patterns in relationships with others, sexuality, self-image, relationships within the family, and the different statements that starvation makes in each situation. Then she can see whether these statements are still relevant and how they can be stated in a different manner.

Another issue to look at is the need for perfection, the need for ultimate statements, for totality in action. Where does this need originate? What would happen if she were not perfect? What would it say about her if she had faults? If she recognizes her humanity and incompleteness and incompetence at times, what would success and failure mean to her, and why does she have to invest her whole being in overcoming any human flaws?

Another important issue to look at is that of punishment and feeding herself. This does not necessarily mean actual food, but any form of nourishment. What is so scary about allowing herself to have, to get, to receive, to be fed and taken care of, without such extreme measures as having to go to hospital or fainting from total weakness? One way of looking at the issue of

Fighting Food

nourishment and feeding is to try to explore with the women in the group what the group means for them. How do they feel about needing a group, being dependent on other people, and actually admitting, in a way, the need for some nourishment? What is the significance of this need to talk with others and of the fact that they need help? This is a very important issue for the anorexic woman, who feels she has to do everything herself and cannot ask for help in a direct way. Explore in the here and now of the group all the fears and feelings around needing others, wanting to get from others, being in the group not just to give but also to receive. Admitting to that will be difficult and will be the first step in acknowledging other needs.

Another issue for the anorexic woman is the mirror and the reflection of herself in it. It is very well known that most anorexic women, however thin they are, still experience themselves as overweight, fat, plump. They are not satisfied with the way they look; even when they are dangerously underweight they feel they are never thin enough. The mirror work may bring the two images closer together. We believe that what the anorexic woman sees reflected to her in the mirror is not just her body, but a symbolic part of herself, that needy, demanding, yearning self which she so desperately tries to kill by starving her body, but which in turn screams out to her: 'I want to be seen, noticed, listened to.' This may be the reason for her still seeing herself as so enormous when really, physically, she is so emaciated. By beginning to acknowledge her needs and at the same time working with the reflection of her body in the mirror, the two may get a bit closer together. She may be able to see herself more realistically.

The issue of good and bad and the split between them is another area to be explored. For the anorexic woman GOOD is the perfect person in her mind, who needs nothing, who is clean of needs, of menstruation, of any mundane human 'dirt'. GOOD is not eating, not asking for anything, not wanting. GOOD is the very well-organized, controlled, familiar woman who has every moment of a given day well planned in advance. GOOD is saying '*no, I do not want*'. GOOD is being independent, individual. BAD is experienced as neediness, greediness, asking for something – all the opposites of GOOD. The woman may need to put what she considers good and bad into more realistic and less extreme opposing positions, and come to realize that we are all human beings with faults and deficiencies, good and bad at the same time; the good and bad need not be so opposing, nor so separate and split from one another.

Structure

Structure is important in groups for bulimic women and compulsive eaters. One of the most important issues for a woman who eats compulsively and for the bulimic woman is the issue of control. She feels out of control in terms of her eating patterns, as though her eating habits are utterly unstructured: no 'proper' meals or specific place for eating or buying food, no regular hours or amounts of food – it is all unexpected, as though someone else is in charge of the situation. Her emotions as well feel shattered, and she constantly needs to quiet them down so that she doesn't feel their depth and strength. Another aspect of the compulsive eater's life is the statement: 'I do not deserve; I will not ask for what I want; I do not deserve any time or attention for myself.'

When these two aspects are put together, what becomes clear is that each group session needs to be structured in such a way that each member gets time for herself, and that each one gets the same amount of time as all the rest of the group. In the therapeutic process in general, the watch plays a large role in terms of boundaries. It is important that the beginning and ending of the sessions are kept strict. The use of the time as well as the acceptance of its boundaries gives a good indication as to how an individual may use and fulfil her time, space, her life in general, and how she may take control and power over this use of time and space. Coming late as well as wanting to stay longer after the end of the session can be interpreted in terms of boundaries, expectations, satisfaction, anger. In many instances the feelings which are not expressed in words during the session itself will be expressed through this 'breaking' of the boundaries. These issues are particularly important for the compulsive eater, who is creating her boundaries through her own body, who has little sense of boundaries, and who can hardly ever ask directly for what she wants or needs. (For a detailed discussion of boundaries and their importance in therapy and in eating problems, see Chapter 7.)

It is therefore very important to give an equal amount of time to each member, even when she does not feel she can fill the whole time with words. Just the understanding that it is her own time, that all attention is focused on what she has to say, and that no one is to interfere with her except in asking questions about what she says, is essential. Often women get anxious and frightened to have time just to be listened to, to have attention, to have space. To allow themselves to relax into feeling that it is all right, permitted, even pleasurable and helpful to be listened to, attended to, given space, is one of the most important as well as the most difficult things to achieve.

With this framework in mind, the group chooses one subject as the issue to work on within the session. Examples might include mother and food; sexuality and eating; relationships with others in connection with eating habits. Usually the subject will have been 'prepared' in advance, and the women will come to the session with some idea of what they are going to say after trying to link some of their experiences with their eating. They then talk about what these connections and feelings may be in the session, and the rest of the group ask questions and point out any connections they notice or any new understanding of the situation. So each member gets a chance to talk about the subject and get feedback from the group. It is this aspect that is so important and new for each individual woman in the group. Thinking about these issues on one's own may be very helpful if one is trying to understand, analyse, make connections. But it is the contribution of other women who may feel similarly or may have gone through the same experiences which can make a difference; this can give a whole new perspective on an event, a whole new understanding of something one may have seen and understood in a limited way for many years.

Obviously this framework is only a suggestion; each group must find the method of working with which they feel most comfortable, and can discuss this as they go along. Some groups find it tiring to have members talk for half an hour each at a time, so they try to give less time or work in a more segmented way. Some groups find that starting with each woman talking for five minutes about how her week has been is quite valuable as a preparation before they start with the actual 'subject' of the session. Some groups find that games, fantasies and exercises give them more insight, so they start with those and move from there to the issue they plan to work on. Working in pairs is another way to save time yet give individual attention to each member; this will give each member some individual attention, and then after that the group can relax and have a more unstructured discussion without necessarily having to keep time or share it equally. Sessions can also be a combination of all of these suggestions.

The structure is therefore very flexible, and women need to find out among themselves which way of working suits them best as a group. There are not many rules about content or structure apart from these. The most important thing is for the members of the group to discuss things as they go along, to be creative and open about changing ways that do not suit them, and to be able to discuss honestly with the other members any problems and techniques that feel irrelevant, difficult or unnecessary.

Structure in groups for anorexic women

Earlier in this chapter we mentioned that anorexic women have certain difficulties working in groups. Different rules are required in self-help groups for compulsive eaters and those for anorexics. In our opinion, the main difference between these two kinds of groups in terms of the structure of the session itself lies in the fact that anorexic groups need a less specific structure, less defined ways of working. The difference between the more defined structure of the compulsive eating group and the free-flowing nature of the anorexic group lies in the nature of these two ways of coping. As the compulsive eater feels out of control and that her life has no structure, and this expresses itself in her pattern of eating, she needs the group to give her some well-defined, controlled structure, a place where she knows she has security, safety, definition. The anorexic, on the other hand, directs her life in a very rigorously structured and controlled manner. The main issue in her life is control, and her day-to-day activities are often under military discipline. The group for the anorexic, therefore, will not need to be so structured and well defined. The safety and security of the group is very important, but the structure within that doesn't have to mean that each member has exactly the same amount of time. It is important that each member has time at some point in the session, as the feeling of deprivation and of not deserving the time and space is immense and difficult to acknowledge. So the boundaries of the group as a whole are very important (starting on time, ending on time, confidentiality, etc.), but with these kept safe, the structure of the session itself can be much more flexible.

As for the issues raised and the ways of dealing with these issues, we believe that they will be much the same. Some specific examples follow in the next chapter.

NOTES

1 S. Ernst and L. Goodison (1981): *In Our Own Hands. A Book of Self-Help Therapy*, The Women's Press, London.

2 S. Orbach (1978): *Fat is a Feminist Issue*, Hamlyn, London.

3 G. Parry-Crooke and J. Ryan (1986): *Evaluation of Self Help Groups for Women with Compulsive Eating Problems*, Health Education Authority, London.

4 W. R. Bion (1968): *Experiences in Groups*, Tavistock, London.

5 G. Parry-Crooke and J. Ryan, ibid.

11
SELF-HELP IN PRACTICE

Before we go on to describe the specific exercises that could be used in the groups at different sessions, it may be useful to look again at some of the issues that we have mentioned earlier in the book and give a brief description of what may be the aims in working with these. These are only brief points, relating to fuller discussions earlier in the book.

Needs: This involves each woman finding out about her own needs and discovering ways to meet them: to respect and acknowledge their existence and not try to substitute for them with food. Needs are present in every area of her life; her task is to learn what they may be in every specific area and understand what it may mean for her to meet them.

Mother–daughter relationships: To find out what in this relationship has been the reason for her 'choosing' this kind of eating behaviour, to try to find out more about issues of separation and individuation within this relationship and what the statements are she is making to her mother through her body. What was the mother's relationship to food, to her own body, to her daughter's body? How does she feature in the issues and conflicts around food?

Sexuality: To find out the attitudes and fears connected with sexuality, intimacy, and relationships with others, and to try to deal with these directly without using the fatness or thinness as an excuse or a protection and the obsession with food as an escape.

Self-image: It is necessary for each woman to understand the origin of her low self-image and really get into the feelings involved, such as disgust, hatred, and revulsion. By understanding and analysing these feelings, talking about them, she can slowly get out the other side, step by step getting to like herself more by getting to know herself, and being more forgiving and accepting of herself and less judgemental. (This is not as easy and simple as it sounds. It is a long and hard struggle. Some exercises are suggested later on in this chapter.)

Dependence: It is important to learn to acknowledge the need to be dependent, the reality of being weak as well as strong, dependent as well as independent, and not to judge the need for dependence as a sign of worthlessness or unacceptability, weakness or stupidity. Dependence is an integral part of our relationships with others (though by no means the only one) and as such is one which is present in our relationships, not something we try to get rid of.

Control: Each woman needs to learn to take control of her life but not through food; she needs to understand that being out of control does not necessarily mean being bad or losing her grip, and that if her life feels out of control, attempting to control her body through losing weight or going on a diet is not the answer. We all have times of chaos, we all have areas in our lives that at times feel as though they are not under control. That does not mean that we are falling apart or that we are bad people. It can be a frightening experience, but one needs to learn to live with a certain level of uncertainty, confusion and not always having everything under control.

Femininity: It is important for each woman to get more in touch with her inner feminine nature, to learn more about her body and her cycles, about what femininity means to her and what fantasies and fears are involved with this issue. She will need to explore her mother's femininity. What messages were conveyed to her both through conversations, behaviour and the model of her mother's feminine nature? What does she feel about this part of her mother's life? Can she identify with it? Who is her model of femininity?

Boundaries: Each woman has to learn about her own boundaries, her power to say 'yes' to what she wants as well as 'no' to what she doesn't want. She has to come to accept her own self and her space and time, and to manage to ask for these and not allow others to step in against her will; to realize that to assert, ask, accept and reject are equally important and are all within her power and absolutely necessary for her well-being.

How it is done: examples of practical work

As well as discussion, self-help groups can and do use a variety of experiential techniques. This is often helpful for enabling women

Self-help in Practice

to be really in touch with feelings, rather than just talking about them. Role plays are often useful, and can create a situation in which the whole group can enter into and understand the experience of a group member. What we call a fantasy is simply a way of inviting the group members to imagine themselves into a situation and see what feelings it produces. The rationale for this kind of work, together with a rich array of possible exercises, is to be found in Sheila Ernst and Lucy Goodison's book, *In Our Own Hands*.[1] It is an invaluable guide to self-help therapy.

With any exercise, fantasy or discussion we use, it is very important to remember that even though the women are there to share a common problem and a common experience, each woman is an individual with her own unique experience and feelings and that fact should be respected. It is very important for each woman to feel that her feelings and experiences are not being judged, even if they are very different from those of some other group members. Her experience should be understood in the context of her own circumstances.

In what follows, we shall suggest how some crucial issues might be tackled by compulsive eaters, anorexics and bulimics in groups.

Needs

Compulsive eating groups

In the groups we find ways of working out what each woman needs in different situations, especially in those where she is driven to food and to eating compulsively. The assumption is that one of the reasons a woman eats compulsively is to fill or cover up needs that are not met, that are not even acknowledged as needs, and which are being 'substituted' or 'compensated' for with food. The initial situation before the 'binge' will given an indication of what those needs are. First of all the woman must recognize the need, then either find a way to answer it or slowly come to understand that food is not really answering it. The nature of life means that sometimes we have to live with and bear the frustrations of not having our needs met. The final step is finding an 'appropriate' way to deal with this frustration.

In order to understand what these needs are in a specific situation, we role-play the situation that preceded a binge, look at the people involved, the interactions that were going on, the emotions that were expressed and those that were not, and the projections and fantasies on the woman's part in this situation. What could she have done in order to meet these needs? If the situation occurs again, what are the alternatives? How can she take the risk of asking for what she wants without being devastated if she is rejected?

If we take a specific situation which occurs in the life of one of the participants that week, different women in the group can role-play different people in the situation described and learn from each other ways to deal with them other than by bingeing. A woman in the group may say to the woman whose situation is played out: 'How could you take this kind of attitude, how can you bear it? I would have tried to stop it, I would have said . . .'

Sometimes, in an attempt to learn more about what our needs are at different times, group members make a list of different needs or emotions and possible options for dealing with them in a way that will be caring for themselves, assertive and satisfying. For example, if I have a need for company at a given time, what can I do about it other than turn to food? Or if I need to relax, or express anger or any other feeling, how can I deal with it directly?

Groups for anorexic women

When working with the issue of needs in a self-help group for anorexics, each woman first has to recognize not only that all humans have needs, but also that in order to live more fully one has to listen and attend to one's needs on all levels (physical, emotional and intellectual).

The group explores with her her fantasy about what would happen if she needed someone or something, about how she feels she might be used, abused or humiliated if she expressed needs, or about what in her fantasy might happen to others if she needed them.

On another level, the group can explore a woman's early experiences with her parents when she expressed her needs. This could be done by asking one of the group members to role-play her mother or father in order to explore the reactions (such as anger, dismissal, silence) she faced when asking for something. Another technique is for her to use a cushion which she can imagine to be her mother. She could sit opposite that cushion and try to talk to it as if it were her mother and she as a child were asking something of her. This may at first be a very difficult and embarrassing exercise to use, especially in front of a whole group. However, after one gets used to this way of working, one can really see the benefits of it as a way to evoke feelings of situations which occurred in the past and which are in our memory only as feelings or sensations, not as a conscious event.

Another area to look at in order to find out what the woman needs and wants are the situations that cause her to crave food, even when she does not actually eat. What these situations mean and who is involved in them are important factors.

Ginny, who had been anorexic for many years, is a good example of a woman who shows great difficulty in expressing her needs. During the last session of a short term group, her eyes started rolling and her head dropped to one side. When questioned about her behaviour and what people could do to help, she answered negatively and insisted on the group going on with the session. Eventually she fainted and fell off her chair. After regaining consciousness, she showed much hostility and anger and pushed everyone away, saying: 'Nothing is going on, it's none of your business, leave me alone.' She dismissed our suggestions that she might feel angry about the group ending. We continued with the session and finally she started crying and expressed some of her distress. She wanted attention, she wanted space, she was intensely angry and distressed about the group ending, but none of these could she acknowledge or express directly.

An exercise that could be used within the group on this issue is to give each member a few moments to say ten sentences starting with 'I need', for example: a cuddle, reassurance, attention, 'Sue to tell me she likes me', 'Sarah to sit next to me'.

Bulimia groups

For the bulimic woman, like the compulsive eater, it is well worth spending time understanding just what it is she needs, what needy feelings she has, when she decides or feels driven to a binge. Bulimic women are aware of having needs, often powerful and frightening needs. The important point is their ambivalence about having those needs seen or attended to.

A fantasy about early experiences with parents may be tried. Go back to any age in your childhood . . . you are frightened

... you need someone to hold you ... you go to your mother, ask for a cuddle ... What is her reaction? Does she cuddle you? What does she say? And most importantly, what feelings are you left with? Many bulimic women experience an enormous sense of anger and humiliation at having needs which are not met.

Mother–daughter relationships
Compulsive eating groups

Here the initial exercise that we suggest is 'mother and food'. Again each woman presents the connections in her own way, bearing in mind questions like: What were the eating patterns at home? How were meal times? Was food a way of expressing emotions? What were they? Did your mother give food as an emotional expression? Did you refuse the food to express your feelings? Were you allowed to eat what you wanted when you wanted, as much as you wanted? Did rejecting food mean rejecting your mother? Try to find out all the different patterns within the family, and then move on to present situations. What is the dynamic and interaction now with your mother around food? What are the messages? What are the statements expressed through accepting or rejecting your mother's food?

Another exercise, similar to the one described earlier, is to talk to a cushion as though it were your mother and tell her all you can't say with words but do say with your attitude to food. Also, try to find out how many of these statements you are using in your own life in your attitude to other people. How much of your mother's relationship to food has passed on to you?

We sometimes use another exercise in order to see how much a mother's concepts of image, beauty, fatness, thinness and should's and ought's affect the compulsive eater, and what her fantasies are about how she can please her mother and what she needs to be in order to do that. In this exercise the women pair up and talk to each other as if each were her own mother talking about her to a friend. Another exercise around this issue can be talking to one's mother on a cushion about one's own childhood, the way the compulsive eater feels about herself, or any other issue that was and is important to her in relation to her mother.

Groups for anorexic women

There are many important questions that should be discussed in the group, when working with this issue:

- What were the relationships of the family members to food?
- What were the rituals around food and eating, at meal times, types of food, ways of serving, conversations around the table?
- What was the atmosphere around the table? Which meals were eaten together? What was important about meals? Who prepared them? Who served them? What were the feelings involved in preparing, serving, eating?
- Was the mother overweight/underweight? Was she very aware of food and weight?
- Who is mother – can you describe her in detail – physical, character, emotion, behaviour?
- How much of you is similar to mother and how much is rebelling against being like her?
- What are the first memories of contact with mother? Did she touch you? How did she feed you? What message did she give with the food?
- How much did mother allow you to be different? How did she react when you behaved in a way she disliked or when you felt differently from her about things or people or situations?
- What did you do at home in order to receive mother's love, attention, and acceptance?
- Can you think of any connection in your family between punishment and food?
- If you failed in exams or at school what was your parents' reaction?

There are several ways these questions could be worked on within the group, either as a discussion or through exercises:

(a) The woman role-plays her mother talking about her daughter to a friend. She talks about her appearance, her personality, her behaviour.
(b) In pairs, tell the story of your mother's life.

(c) A fantasy: same principle as the one on p. 163 about the film maker: on one screen appears an ideal mother, and on the other – your own mother. In the fantasy, compare how the ideal mother reacts to her daughter with how your own mother reacts in the following situations – holding her daughter, taking her for a walk, feeding her, talking with her, mother's reaction to a naughty deed, and any other situation that you feel in the group is relevant.

You will notice that for the anorexia groups we are making rather more detailed suggestions for the questions which might be asked. This is because anorexic women often find it particularly difficult to focus on the emotional content of an issue and to find words for their feelings.

Bulimia groups

Relationships with mothers and fathers have emerged as a powerful theme in our groups. This is often a painful area and needs to be approached with great sensitivity. We find that deprivation or the idea of deprivation is an important factor in bulimia. It emerges often as a feeling of having been denied a real understanding and as a withholding of good things from the parents. At the same time, parents may be felt to be over-controlling and intrusive. Issues that could be explored include:

Mother's and father's ambivalence in their attitudes towards you. Were they consistent or inconsistent in their attitudes and reactions?

Feelings of deprivation as a child. What were your parents' attitudes to food? To femininity? To sexuality?

Sexuality

Compulsive eating groups

This is one of the important issues dealt with through compulsive eating. In it is involved the reality of each woman's sexual life. Is she in a relationship? How is sex in this relationship? How do eating compulsively and being fat come into the picture? Do they serve any purpose? What investment do they carry? Are there any correlations between sex and bingeing?

We dedicate a few sessions to dealing with this issue; in one of them the subject is 'food and sexuality', and each woman finds her own way of addressing the issue for herself. We try to find out the fears and fantasies involved, the taboos and meanings conveyed to each woman in an overt or covert way from family, teachers and others. An example could be: Try to remember the first conversation your mother or father had with you about sex – if they did or did not explain anything (the absence means a lot). What were your fantasies or conclusions as a result? What is forbidden? What is allowed? Try with the feeling of that little girl that you were to recognize what this secret entity is; what does it mean?

We try to cover situations where sexuality becomes an issue, such as parties, intimate relationships, and, by means of fantasy, role play and cushion work (as mentioned above) with boyfriend or mother or father; to find out the details and fears involved. For example, if a woman is scared of sexual advances from men or women at a party, of their opinion of her, of their intentions towards her – what is the fear about, what is its origin? What would happen if she did agree to these advances? What would it say about her? What protection or ways of dealing with it can she discover?

Groups for anorexic women

The fears and conflicts around sexuality in terms of beliefs, performance, relationships, intimacy should be discussed. The discussion could be centred around the woman's first experiences with menstruation, sexual intercourse, her first conversation about sex, sexual education (who was it given by? when?). What were the attitudes of others towards sex as she understood them? Who (if anyone) explained to her about menstruation? What was the attitude conveyed? How did she feel about it? Can she find any connection between food and sexuality? What here follows is a fantasy that could be used – with variations as appropriate – in working within the group on a variety of issues.

The fantasy You are a film maker. You sit in a cinema all on your own in front of two tables. You are the writer of the story, the director, the one responsible for the creation of this film in all its detail. On each one of the tables there is a projector. On the wall in front of you there are two screens on which the films will be projected. Remember everything in this film is in your hands, up to you.

On the right-hand screen appears a thin woman. She is walking towards you. She is the heroine of this film, and you are creating the story of her life. Who is she? What is her job? What is her background, what is her family like? Is she married? How is her social life? Who are her friends? What does she do in her free time? Where is she going? Where is she coming from? What does she look like? Who does she live with? Is she on her own? With a lover? How is her sex life? Does she go on holidays? Where to? Try to describe every detail in her life, all aspects you can cover about her social life, her relationships, her job, and any other aspect you can think of.

Then, on the left-hand side, appears a fat woman. Describe her life in the same way, with the same details.

Bulimia groups

Many bulimic women appear to cope with their sexuality quite well. They often manage to have sexual relationships (sometimes several at the same time), and in a superficial way may find these relationships satisfying. The problem, however, is that because of her feelings of being bad inside, the bulimic woman is likely to have feelings of disgust and fear about her body, both inside and outside, which are difficult for her to acknowledge and be conscious of. The task in the group is to enable some of these less conscious feelings to emerge.

For women who are very concerned about weight and who may only feel able to have sexual relationships when they are thin, the film maker fantasy may help. It is likely that all the negative feelings about sexuality will be attached to the fat woman. The important point for discussion in the group is which image the woman herself actually identifies with.

Another way of approaching the issue is to examine the extent to which women in the group are really able to use their sexuality for their own pleasure and satisfaction. Very often it emerges that more often women use their sexuality to prove to themselves and others that they are 'OK'.

Self-image

Compulsive eating groups

The very low image overweight women have of themselves is

centred around their bodies and being fat and unattractive. Very low self-esteem is reflected in their total ignorance of their bodies. They rarely look at their bodies in the mirror, and even less often in a loving and appreciative manner. The aim in this area is first for women to learn to look at their bodies, to acknowledge that they have a body and to get to know it with all its parts and limbs, and second to learn to look at it with a more positive and accepting eye and really feel that 'This is my body and I have to look at all of it, see what I like and what I dislike in it, and try to learn to accept the parts I do not like, or at least to have knowledge of them and not just dismiss the whole as horrible.'

For this we use mirror work, where the women are asked to devote some time at home on their own, in a relaxed way, just to looking at their bodies in front of the mirror and getting to know them better.

We also have a session in which we talk about our bodies and the parts of them we like. We try to get at the feelings involved and to discover the symbolism and meaning of the parts we dislike as well as those we like.

Another exercise is for the woman to draw herself at present and also as she would like to look. The way the page is used is symbolic of the way she uses her own space and time. The drawings, therefore, can show how much of her space she actually uses or how much she feels she takes up. If any limbs have been left out, omitted from the drawing, their absence and the meaning of that specific limb missing is very important and could indicate how much it has been used or feared or absent in her life. Whether a woman draws herself clothed or naked is also important – her position, her face, her expression, the feeling of the drawing, the message in her posture, the most prominent part of the body, the most vivid or energetic part of the body and what these mean in terms of the reality of her life. In terms of the comparison between the two drawings, the same applies: where is the energy centred in both, and if in different places, what does this difference mean *for her*?

Other than this, we encourage a woman to find ways to treat herself – by having relaxing baths, buying new clothes or doing other nice things for herself, trying to learn to respect and give to herself in ways other than eating, as well as through food she enjoys when she is really hungry. Slowly, on all levels, she must learn to give herself time, space and respect, starting from the group where people listen to what she says. She has her own time and space within the group and may be able to listen more to herself, to her body, and maybe through that to give more care to herself.

Groups for anorexic women

The issues to be discussed here are the anorexic's feelings about her body, attitudes in her family to thin/fat, attitudes of different members of her family towards her body, her own feelings around fat (disgust, fear, hate). This could be done through exercises such as looking in the mirror without the fierce judgement of fat/thin or good/bad, but for the woman just to watch the different parts of her body and slowly learn the lines of her shape without harsh criticism. This will not be done until quite late on in the life of the group, as it is a very threatening exercise for a woman who is anorexic and a shift in this aspect of her problem will only occur after some basic work has been done on other issues.

Another exercise: 'My ideal woman' – someone you would describe as the ideal woman in your eyes. Describe her in detail. The group can help with questions and remarks about different aspects of the description. Or: draw yourself as you feel you look after a few days of fasting and on another page after a big meal and compare the two drawings.

Or: the first time you remember making a conscious decision not to eat. What were the circumstances, describe the situation and the people involved.

Or: what would a conversation sound like between your 'mind' and your body. Here is an example:

M. to B.: 'You imprison me with all these silly things I have to do for you. You tie me down, you limit me.'

B. to M.: 'You never give me what I want. You do not treat me nicely, always carry me around with no respect or consideration. You don't even know me well enough. You exhaust me and expect me to work so hard at being thin.'

Bulimia groups

In groups for bulimic women it is important to consider the way in which self-image, and in particular body-image, changes. Drawing can again be a useful tool. In this case, we would suggest that women are asked to draw themselves as they are most of the time, the way they feel they look after a binge and a third drawing of 'me after vomiting'.

Again, it is important to look at the drawing in detail, to notice the facial expressions, the position of hands and feet, as well as the size and shape of the body. A woman may draw a picture of herself as much thinner and more attractive after she has vomited; it is also important to notice whether she looks happy and what her whole demeanour conveys about the kind of person she is. You may well find that her body-image (how attractive her body is) frequently contradicts her fuller self-image (how attractive or 'good' she is as a person).

Working with dynamics within the group

Dynamics within the group can, and we feel should, be understood and worked with in two ways. At one level, we have the here-and-now situation of feelings and responses between the two members of the group. At another level is what each of them brings to the group from her own past which may contribute to her feeling the way she does.

For example, a woman may get angry at another woman who constantly complains in the group and thereby gets extra attention. At the level of the here-and-now her anger is about the whining, the manipulation and her own jealousy of the attention the other woman gets. But there may also be another level that needs to be explored. It may be, for example, that her own sister at home got all the attention through constantly complaining. This means that she is still carrying the unresolved anger, jealousy and hatred from her own family and is projecting it on to someone who repeats the same pattern in the group.

Obviously, working with this in the group creates a lot of problems, which is why it is not often done in self-help groups.

In a group without a leader, women will find it difficult to separate their feelings for and projections upon each other. As women we listen to others' emotions before listening to our own. Therefore it is quite difficult to listen to our own feelings and to own them. We keep projecting them out and deal with them out there in the relationship with other people.

In a group of women with no therapy experience and no

leader, it can be quite difficult to separate all these feelings and to recognize whether they are really in the here-and-now or carried from the past. This is made more complicated by the fact that we invariably do project our own unresolved feelings from the past on to people in the present who remind us of those figures from the past and who thus do actually affect us in the here-and-now.

Another problem is the same issue – if much time is spent working on the issues between the members of the group, there will not be enough time to deal with the subject of compulsive eating, and it may divert the emphasis from the more important work and create an imbalance, as well as being a way to avoid working with difficult issues around eating and the meaning of fat.

Another difficulty could be that members of the group find it difficult to express in a direct and honest way feelings that concern other members of the group. For example, expressing anger, irritation, impatience, etc. are 'not on' in a group situation, especially in a group of women and more so in a group of compulsive eaters. It is easier to talk about someone's anger towards her mother who is not present than to actually express anger towards another member of the group and work on that. A woman often finds it difficult to express emotions she experiences in the here-and-now towards another woman in the group (especially if it is a 'negative, unacceptable emotion') in an honest and open way.

One valuable way of helping women to become aware of dynamics within the group would be to look at the dynamics and projections that occur between the group members and to see how what happens in the group relates to the experiences of the women involved. This could be looked at in terms of past experiences in the family – patterns of eating and using food for emotional expression – as well as current behaviour with others outside of the group. A woman needs to have some awareness of the clues in the attitudes and relationships in the group to discover who these other women represent for her, how she can relate to them through these projections, and what patterns she can notice in her own behaviour that are similar to the ones she had at home.

In one of the groups, Pat was talking about how horrible she felt about herself. She expressed deep feelings of emotional inadequacy, loneliness and despair about the way she was. Her sadness came across strongly, with sobbing and tears. When she became particularly upset, another woman from the group – Julie – went over, gave her a hug around her head (the position Pat was in didn't allow Julie to hug her with full contact) and said, 'Come, come, now, it's all right, do not cry now, everything will be all right. It's not so bad, you are really a beautiful person.'

Julie definitely wanted to give Pat something. The way many parents deal with children crying is to give them a sweet and a pat on the head: 'Have a sweet and it's going to be all right, just stop crying.' Even if done in a warm and loving way, this is quite a destructive way to deal with the child's pain. It is distracting her from what is painful so that she forgets, but it is not really dealing with what she feels bad about and what the pain is about, or allowing her to experience the depth of pain she is feeling and stay with it. At the same time, it conveys the 'understanding' that a sweet will always heal the pain. More often than not, this impulse comes from the parent being unable to stand the child's pain because of his or her own pain or sadnesss that has not been dealt with, and the over-identification the parent feels as a result. This happens often in the groups. When working further, we had to allow Pat to get into the details of why, what, how, she felt, and give her the space to feel the 'bad' feelings and understand them with our support and warmth as the ground for this work.

On the other hand, we also needed to look at what Julie did – how this was a pattern in her life and affected her personality. It showed what she needed in order to be able to stand Pat's pain as well as get into her own.

We feel that it is an important part of the work to look at the relationships that are formed in the group and to try to learn from these about the way we relate in general to other people, as well as to trace the origins of these ways of behaving in the family. The women in the group are not 'chosen' according to factors like age, size, etc. – there is a great likelihood that the age differences, attitudes, manners, will vary a lot in each group, and this is a potent ground for the women to 'hook' their images of a mother on to an older woman or of a daughter on to a younger woman and relate to them accordingly. Through their projected image on to the other person, much could be learnt about these initial relationships and the way this is dealt with in the group could be helpful in understanding and realizing, step by step, the choice to change. This is important, as we claim that most of our patterns of feeling and behaving come from the initial family relationship and the opportunity to experience and explore these in reality in the group as a form of projection makes it more difficult to intellectualize or distort the experiences as they occur in reality. Issues like competition, boundaries, separation, dependence, will emerge in the group and could well be learnt from in this way.

We recognize the fact that projections occur on 'blind spots', meaning that a person will project her own feelings unknowingly and usually around the most painful or unresolved issues in her life. A person will get angry, sad or disgusted at someone who touches that unresolved issue within her. This usually creates a difficulty in recognizing the issue that needs to be worked on, and in actually working on that issue. However, with awareness of all the difficulties, we do believe that working with the dynamics is an important and potent ground to work from within the group.

NOTES

1 S. Ernst and L. Goodison (1981): *In Our Own Hands. A Book of Self-Help Therapy*, The Women's Press, London.

For a helpful account of self-help compulsive eating groups, see K. Noble, 'Self-help groups: The Agony and the Ecstasy', in M. Lawrence (ed.) (1987): *Fed Up and Hungry*, The Women's Press, London.

Finding help

By now, we hope to have convinced you that eating disorders are not mysteries and they do not occur by chance. They are problems which are meaningful and can be understood. We have also attempted to give you the flavour of what psychotherapeutic help can be like and of the potential of self-help. We would now like to help you think about finding help for yourself.

This is a difficult subject to approach. It would be wonderful if we lived in an ideal world, where there was one 'right' kind of help for eating disorders, which was freely available to everyone. In truth, there is no one kind of help which suits everyone, and many people's choice of treatment is limited by what happens to be available in their area. But before going on to look at the external issues which affect your decisions, we should also acknowledge that there are internal problems about making the decision to seek help and following it through.

Having reached this point in the book, you will be very well aware that people with eating disorders find it very difficult to ask for help. Indeed, eating disorders very often develop in order to cover up and conceal an initial need for help. It sometimes happens that having once read a book about your problem and thus understood a little more about it, you may be tempted to believe that you can now tackle it alone. You should ask yourself if this is actually realistic. Perhaps you have told yourself this before?

Reading a book about eating disorders is a step forward – but it is probably not the decisive one. Perhaps you could make a resolution to at least tell someone about your problem.

In Britain, in order to be referred to a medical specialist, you will have to talk to your general practitioner and ask for a referral. Many family doctors are interested in eating disorders and knowledgeable about local resources. However, don't expect too much. Remember that your GP cannot be an expert on everything, and it may be as well to find out as much as you can before you go.

Fighting Food

Write to the Eating Disorders Association, who have a list of National Health Service resources in your area, as well as counsellors offering private treatment.

If you are offered in-patient treatment and feel that you need this kind of help, ask exactly what kind of help the particular hospital offers. What is their attitude to weight? Do they prescribe drugs? What kind of support can they offer after you leave hospital? It can be difficult to ask these kinds of questions and to be clear about what you want, but it is vital that you feel you have made an active commitment to any treatment you have.

You may feel that you don't want to talk to a doctor and prefer to seek counselling in a non-medical setting. There are a number of voluntary organizations offering counselling and therapy. 'Relate' (formerly the Marriage Guidance Council) is one which has long experience of treating eating disorders. Your local Citizens Advice Bureau will have names of other local organizations.

You may have to be persistent in order to find the kind of help you feel you want.

Self-help

Remember that self-help does not mean struggling on on your own. It means sharing with others who have a similar problem. Whatever professional help you might decide to seek, you may also wish to write to the Eating Disorders Association to find out if there is a self-help group in your area. They also produce helpful literature and stock a wide selection of books on eating disorders.

A word to parents and friends

We are often asked by family members and friends for advice on how to help someone suffering from an eating disorder. Mothers in particular often believe that there is a 'right' way of responding to their daughter – and they just want to know what it is!

There are no rules, and there is no way of being right in such a situation.

Perhaps the most important thing to remember is that you cannot cure your daughter. Parents, friends and teachers can be very helpful in the process of recovery, but almost certainly the sufferer needs outside help.

Finding help

The second point is that feeling guilty will help no one. We all feel guilty when our children are in trouble, but equally most of us also know that we have done our very best, within our own limitations. Your child needs your help desperately now, and feeling guilty is not the best place to start.

If you feel sure she needs help, tell her so. But don't expect that she will immediately agree with you. Try to understand the world from her point of view, but then speak to her from yours. You are very different people, but perhaps at this moment you can be allies. She will need your support in finding the help and the strength to recover.

If you have a family member with an eating disorder, you are in for a stormy time. There will be tears and angry words and you will sometimes feel like giving up. It is very important to remember that love and hate can and do coexist and that words really don't do any lasting damage.

Try not to nag about food all the time; it doesn't do any good. On the other hand, don't feel you have to hide your concern for her health. You may be more in touch with reality than she is. And don't worry all the time about saying the wrong thing. You would be superhuman if you didn't. If you happen to say something which you think has been hurtful, say so. Tell her you sometimes find it difficult to respond helpfully. Then forget about it. Don't go away feeling guilty. You really haven't done anything terrible.

Finally, try to take care of yourself. We have met many family members, especially mothers, who have become so anxious and exhausted that they themselves have become ill with the responsibility of it all. You cannot possibly be responsible for everyone in your family and you must look after yourself. Make a conscious attempt to find some help for yourself; perhaps a friend who is not too involved with the family, or a counsellor. Remember that the Eating Disorders Association is concerned about you as well as your daughter, and that you deserve help too. Be patient. Eating disorders usually reflect a long history of things silently going wrong. It takes time to recover. But you should also be hopeful and optimistic. There will be ups and downs, but with the right kind of help you have every reason to expect your daughter to get better.

Resources

Eating Disorders Association
Sackville Place
44 Magdalen Street
Norwich
Norfolk
(Tel: 0603 621414)

The Women's Therapy Centre
6 Manor Gardens
London N7

BIBLIOGRAPHY

Abraham, S., and Llewellyn-Jones, D. (1984): *Eating Disorders and The Facts*, Oxford University Press, Oxford.

Bell, R. M. (1985): *Holy Anorexia*, University of Chicago Press, Chicago and London.

Boskind-Lodahl, M. (1976): 'Cinderella's Stepsisters: A Feminist Perspective on Anorexia and Bulimia', *Signs: Journal of Women in Culture and Society*, 2, 342–56.

Boskind-White, M., and White, W. C. (1983): *Bulimiarexia. The Binge/Purge Cycle*, Norton, New York, London.

Bruch, H. (1974): *Eating Disorders*, Routledge & Kegan Paul, London.

Bruch, H. (1978): *The Golden Cage*, Open Books, Wells.

Brumberg, J. (1988): *Fasting Girls*, Harvard University Press, Cambridge, Mass.

Chasseguet-Smirgel, J. (1985): *Creativity and Perversion*, Free Association Books, London.

Chernin, K. (1983): *Womansize. The Tyranny of Slenderness*, The Women's Press, London.

Chernin, K. (1986): *The Hungry Self*, Virago, London.

Coward, R. (1984): *Female Desire*, Paladin, London.

Crisp, A. H. (1980): *Anorexia Nervosa. Let Me Be*. Academic Press, London.

Dana, M., and Lawrence, M. (1987): *Women's Secret Disorder*, Grafton, London.

Davis, M., and Wallbridge D. (1983): *Boundary and Space: An Introduction to the Work of D. W. Winnicott*, Penguin, Harmondsworth.

Douglas, M. (1966): *Purity and Danger*, Routledge & Kegan Paul, London.

Ehrenreich, B., and English D. (1979): *For Her Own Good*, Pluto Press, London.

Eichenbaum, L., and Orbach, S. (1983): *Understanding Women*, Penguin, Harmondsworth.

Ernst, S., and Goodison, L. (1981): *In Our Own Hands. A Book of Self-Help Therapy*, The Women's Press, London.

Ernst, S., and Maguire, M. (1987): *Living with the Sphinx*, The Women's Press, London.

Fairbairn, W. R. D. (1952): *Psychoanalytic Studies of the Personality*, Routledge & Kegan Paul, London.

Flax, J. (1981): 'The Conflict between Nurturance and Autonomy', in Howell, E., and Bayes, M (eds.), Basic Books, New York.

Graham, H. (1984): *Women, Health and the Family*, Harvester Press, Brighton.

Guntrip, H. (1968): *Schizoid Phenomena, Object Relations and the Self*, The Hogarth Press, London.

Klein, M. (1937): 'Love, Guilt and Reparation' in Klein, M., and Riviere, J. (eds.), *Love, Hate and Reparation*, The Hogarth Press, London.

Klein, M. (1975): *Envy and Gratitude and other Works*. The Hogarth Press, London.

Kohon, G. (ed.) (1986): *The British School of Psychoanalysis. The Independent Tradition*, Free Association Books, London.

Lawrence, M. (1979): 'Anorexia Nervosa: The Control Paradox', *Women's Studies International Quarterly*, 2, 93–101.

Lawrence, M. (1981): 'Anorexia Nervosa: The Counsellor's Role', *British Journal of Guidance and Counselling*, 9, 74–85.

Lawrence, M. (1984): *The Anorexic Experience*, The Women's Press, London.

Lawrence, M. (1984): 'Education and Identity: Thoughts on the Social Origins of Anorexia', *Women's Studies International Forum* 7, 4, 201–9.

Lawrence, M. (ed.) (1987): *Fed Up and Hungry*, The Women's Press, London.

Lawrence, M. (1987): 'Anorexia and Bulimia: A Psychotherapeutic Approach', *British Review of Bulimia and Anorexia Nervosa*, 1, 2.

Macleod, S. (1981): *The Art of Starvation*, Virago, London.

Mitchell, J. (1986): *The Selected Melanie Klein*, Penguin, Harmondsworth.

Orbach, S. (1978): *Fat is a Feminist Issue*, Hamlyn, London.

Orbach, S. (1984): *Fat is a Feminist Issue 2*, Hamlyn, London.

Orbach, S. (1986): *Hunger Strike*, Faber, London.

Palmer, R. L. (2nd edition 1988): *Anorexia Nervosa*, Penguin, Harmondsworth.

Roche, L. (1984): *Glutton for Punishment*, Pan, London.

Roth, G. (1984): *Breaking Free*, Grafton Books, London.

Roth, G. (1986): *Feeding the Hungry Heart*, Grafton Books, London.

Showalter, E. (1987): *The Female Malady. Women, Madness and English Culture, 1830–1980*, Virago, London.

Wardle, J. (1986): Paper to British Psychological Society, reported in the *Observer*, 6 April 1986.

Welldon, E. V. (1988): *Mother, Madonna, Whore*. Free Association Books, London.

Winnicott, D. W. (1965): *The Maturational Processes and the Facilitating Environment*, The Hogarth Press, London.

Winnicott, D. W. (1971): *Playing and Reality*, Tavistock, London.

Winnicott, D. W. (1975): *Through Paediatrics to Psychoanalysis*, The Hogarth Press, London.

Woodman, M. (1980): *The Owl Was a Baker's Daughter. Obesity, Anorexia Nervosa and the Repressed Feminine*, Inner City Books, Canada.

INDEX

Abraham, S., 37
advertising, 71
aims, of self-help compulsive eating groups, 145
aims, of self-help anorexia groups, 148
agoraphobia, 86
ambivalence, 82, 83
amphetamines, 105
anima, 64
anorexia, 17–29
    and adolescent conflicts, 22
    and control, 69
    and regression, 24
    as a defence, 109
'anorexic family', 24
asceticism, 8–9
autonomy, 81, 84

Baker Miller, J., 77, 95, 96
basic assumption groups, 141
behaviour modification, 108
    dangers of, 108
Bell, R., 8
black women, ix
body image, 60–62
boundaries, 92–101, 155
    in therapy, 131
    within families, 100
Bruch, H., 80, 108, 109
bulimia, 44–54
    and families, 49–50
    and weight control, 44
    physical consequences, 123

chaotic eating, 127
chaos, internal, 127
Chernin, K., 70, 71
Chesler, P., 89

childhood, 76–7, 79–86, 100–101, 160–62
Clarke, M. G., 10
compulsive eating, 30–43
    and competition, 33, 44
    and deprivation, 37
    and fullness, 33
    and guilt, 32
    and hunger, 30
control, 63–70, 156
confidentiality, 135
coping, 46
creativity, 51–2

dependence, 85–8, 155
    on food, 87
deprivation, 37
dieting, 36–8
diets, 103
Dinnerstein, D., 70
disorder, 53, 68
drugs, 105, 108

Eating Disorders Association, 135, 148
eating disorders
    incidence of, 9
    history of, 7
    in men, vii
    as metaphors, 12–15
    physical effects of, 6, 121–4
    and race, 10
Eichenbaum, L., 80, 94
Ernst, S., 85, 140, 142, 157

false boundaries, 94
family
    boundaries in, 100
    in anorexia, 24–6

Index

therapy, 110
fasting, 27
fat
    attitudes to, 60
    disowning of, 62
    unconscious need for, 62, 104
Fat is a Feminist Issue, 11, 34, 35, 59, 72, 143
father–daughter relationship, 83–4
father, separation from, 84
fear of intimacy, 53–4
fear of thinness, 146
femininity, 64–8, 156
food
    forbidden, 33
    industry, 4
    propaganda, 58
    women and, 58

gastric bypass, 106
glamour, 17
good and bad, 50–51, 150
Goodison, L., 157
group dynamics, 140
    in self-help groups, 142, 167–70
group therapy, 131
Gull, Sir W., 8, 107

Health Education Council, 143
Holy Anorexia, 8
hidden part of the self, 98
hospitals, working in, 132
hospitalization, 108, 110

In Our Own Hands, 157
Indian women, 23
infant feeding, 76
institutions, 132
internal world, 116

jaw wiring, 106
Jejunojejunostomy, 106

Jekyll and Hyde, 50

Lasegue, C., 8
laxatives, 1, 6, 121
leaving the group, 139
Llewellyn Jones, D., 37

management of symptoms, 120–21
Mary Magdalen, 74
matriarchal societies, 64
meeting place for self-help groups, 137
men, eating disorders in, vii
menstruation, 65–6
mess, 48, 51–73
    and femininity, 67
metaphor, eating disorders as, 12
Monroe, Marilyn, 71
mothers (of children with eating disorders), 172–3
mother–daughter relationship, 79–83, 155, 160–62
    in anorexia, 24
motherhood, 57

needs, 77–9, 155, 156–60
nurturing, 57

Of Woman Born, 74
Orbach, S., 11, 59, 72, 80, 94, 143
order, 53
Outside In, Inside Out, 94
Owl was a Baker's Daughter, The, 66

Palmer, R. L., 10
parents, 172–3
Parry-Crooke, G., 140, 143
passivity, 64, 86
Perls, F., 93
projection, 140, 169–70
psychology
    of eating disorders, 76–7
psychotherapy, 116–32

psychotherapy *contd*
   resistance to, 117–18

race and eating disorders, 10, 100
racism, ix, 60
Redgrove, P., 65
Rich, A., 74
Ryan, J., 140, 143

secrets, 64
self-denial, 69, 97
self-hatred, 45
self-help, 133
   research on, 143
self-image, 59–60, 155, 164–7
   in anorexia, 63
   in bulimia, 63–4
separation, 85–7
setting up a group, 144
sexual abuse, 101
sexuality, 89–90, 155, 162–4
Shuttle, P., 65
Slade, R., 9
'slimmers' disease', 20
social class, ix, 2, 10, 100
structure, in self-help groups, 151, 153
Surrey, J., 96

target weight, 108, 111
themes, in self-help groups, 137
time-limited groups, 129

time-sharing, in self-help groups, 136
therapeutic relationship, 116, 124–5
therapist's feelings, 119–20
therapy as feeding, 118–19
treatment, 103–14
   cost of, 114
   psychotherapeutic, 116–32
Twiggy, 71

Understanding Women, 80

Victorian era, 11
Virgin Mary, 74
vomiting, 14, 48, 88, 98, 129

weight gain, in anorexia, 108–10, 121–2
whore, 74
Winnicott, D. W., 52, 76, 93
Wise Wound, The, 65
women and food, 58
Women and Madness, 89
women's
   bodies, 65, 70–74; social perceptions of, 60–61, 70–75
   groups, 142 (*see also* self-help)
   magazines, 59, 72
   social status, 56
Women's Therapy Centre, vii, 87, 133
Woodman, M., 66

FOR THE BEST IN PAPERBACKS, LOOK FOR THE

In every corner of the world, on every subject under the sun, Penguin represents quality and variety – the very best in publishing today.

For complete information about books available from Penguin – including Puffins, Penguin Classics and Arkana – and how to order them, write to us at the appropriate address below. Please note that for copyright reasons the selection of books varies from country to country.

In the United Kingdom: Please write to *Dept E.P., Penguin Books Ltd, Harmondsworth, Middlesex, UB7 0DA*

If you have any difficulty in obtaining a title, please send your order with the correct money, plus ten per cent for postage and packaging, to *PO Box No 11, West Drayton, Middlesex*

In the United States: Please write to *Dept BA, Penguin, 299 Murray Hill Parkway, East Rutherford, New Jersey 07073*

In Canada: Please write to *Penguin Books Canada Ltd, 2801 John Street, Markham, Ontario L3R 1B4*

In Australia: Please write to the *Marketing Department, Penguin Books Australia Ltd, P.O. Box 257, Ringwood, Victoria 3134*

In New Zealand: Please write to the *Marketing Department, Penguin Books (NZ) Ltd, Private Bag, Takapuna, Auckland 9*

In India: Please write to *Penguin Overseas Ltd, 706 Eros Apartments, 56 Nehru Place, New Delhi, 110019*

In the Netherlands: Please write to *Penguin Books Netherlands B.V., Postbus 195, NL–1380AD Weesp*

In West Germany: Please write to *Penguin Books Ltd, Friedrichstrasse 10–12, D–6000 Frankfurt/Main 1*

In Spain: Please write to *Longman Penguin España, Calle San Nicolas 15, E–28013 Madrid*

In Italy: Please write to *Penguin Italia s.r.l., Via Como 4, I-20096 Pioltello (Milano)*

In France: Please write to *Penguin Books Ltd, 39 Rue de Montmorency, F-75003 Paris*

In Japan: Please write to *Longman Penguin Japan Co Ltd, Yamaguchi Building, 2–12–9 Kanda Jimbocho, Chiyoda-Ku, Tokyo 101*